THE ART OF MANUFACTURING DEVELOPMENT

ART OF
CTURING
OPMENT

lric Bolling

chanical Engineering
tor of the
ms Engineering Program
Michigan–Dearborn

y Chris Chesley

ower

Published by
Gower Publishing Limited
Gower House
Croft Road
Aldershot
Hampshire GU11 3HR
England

Gower
Old Post Road
Brookfield
Vermont 05036
USA

G. Fredric Bolling has asserted his right under the Copyright,
Designs and Patents Act 1988 to be identified as the author of this
work.

British Library Cataloguing in Publication Data
Bolling, G. Fredric
  Art of Manufacturing Development
  I. Title
  658.5
  ISBN 0–566–07463–X

Library of Congress Cataloging-in-Publication Data
Bolling, G. Fredric.
    The art of manufacturing development / G. Fredric Bolling.
      p.   cm.
    ISBN 0–566–07463–X
    1. Production engineering. 2. Production planning. I. Title.
  TS176.B639   1994
  658.5—dc20   94–7889
                                                             CIP

Typeset in 11 point Baskerville by Photoprint, Torquay, Devon and
printed in Great Britain by Hartnolls Ltd, Bodmin.

This book is dedicated to

The Ford Motor Company
and to my friends and teachers there

and

to my wife

Valerie Ann Withington

CONTENTS

ARE THERE ANY OTHER RULES?

LIST OF FIGURES

PREFACE

An **art** may be defined as: **the conscious use of a skill acquired by experience, study or observation combined with creative imagination.** This book and others in a companion series attempt to describe skills, needed for work to be done in several technical areas, that are themselves not technical in nature. The reader is warned that a considerable number of pages is used up to establish a mood for each book, before either the skills or the art itself become clear, much less obvious. Perhaps a defensive statement like this is needed when you describe an art which is qualitative, in contrast to a skill or science which is quantitative.

In this particular volume attention is paid to the people who do the job of manufacturing development, to their attitudes and perseverence and to the way they use their individual technical knowledge. Only after these people and their successes are described can their skills and imagination be combined to define **the art of manufacturing development**.

Acknowledgements

I would like to thank Chris Chesley for providing the sketches, and Gillian Pines who painstakingly checked my early draft manuscripts.

THREE PRESCRIPTIONS FOR SUCCESS

Some first things

This book tells you why some people and some development projects are successful. The observations are based on real (but past) projects, associated with the Manufacturing Development Center (MDC) of the Ford Motor Company, as described in the words of people I worked with.

For reasons which will become clear, the focus is on success and not on failure or, as many people suggest, on recognizing the reasons for failures so you can avoid repeating them. The result of studying successes yields two of three prescriptions, one about the conditions that must obtain in order for success to be achieved, and the other about the characteristics of successful developers. Given freedom, challenge and time, these conditions and these people can be put together.

As I worked, seeing both success and failure in my endeavors and in those of my friends, it was natural to ask what are the conditions for success in a project. It was also natural to ask who are the people who can achieve success. The first question wasn't easy to answer and the second question doesn't have a direct answer at all, so the answer I will provide may seem oblique. I will contend that the successful practitioners of manufacturing development are Masters of an art, much like Zen Masters are masters of the way of Zen.

The working title of this book was *Zen In The Art of Manufacturing Development*, but the overworked use of the titles like this and the sometimes quirky nature of books with titles using the word "Zen" persuaded me to avoid the choice. However, I remain convinced that manufacturing development is an art: I want to make this connection for you; and I want to describe the what, the how-to and the who of this art.

I was involved with a full spectrum of manufacturing development for nearly a decade. During that time, whenever someone asked me what I did, I generally responded with "I'm in manufacturing," and then if they asked "what in particular?" or some such question, I responded with "manufacturing development". The questioning usually stopped there. Not because the askers knew what it was, but probably because they felt they should, and would betray ignorance if they had asked "well, what is that?"

Most of us who have worked in manufacturing development have to be pleased that this sort of questioning falls short. It is very difficult to say what manufacturing development is. That is another reason for this book – to explain the difficulty and to define manufacturing development.

◆　◆

The reference to Ford a few paragraphs back is very important for me. Even though I had an extensive formal education, lasting more than twenty years, Ford has been my best teacher. I started in research and traveled into research planning, product planning, purchasing, and product development, followed by a stint in Ford of Europe and interspersed by some special/peculiar assignments. Finally, I became director of the Manufacturing Development Center (MDC).

This activity was organizationally relocated four times while I was director and was probably restructured twice as many times in its earlier years. Of course, there were very good reasons for each change, but I suspect that few members of company managements who are parties to reorganizations genuinely know what operations like manufacturing development or other similar groups really are. They are quite properly interested primarily in the end results. So who does know about manufacturing development?

The people inside a successful organization know. This doesn't mean that they will talk about it easily, because success is elusive and you can damn success by publicly acknowledging its existence. Fortunately, I was able to persuade these friends of mine to talk. I will start straight away with one of their voices, telling you about an example of what is done in this art.

The plant problem

Two of my former co-workers, Al Oros and Fred Sawyer were winners of the Henry Ford Technological Award in 1988 along with Paul DeJager of Transmission and Chassis Division "for conceiving and developing an innovative manufacturing process for welding aluminium driveshafts". Here is a description, mostly in Al Oros's words, of what these gentlemen developed.

Background

As a part of mid-1980s vehicle weight reduction programs, Ford Powertrain Engineering designed an aluminium driveshaft which was put into production at the Ford Sterling plant. This driveshaft was manufactured by joining the yoke to the driveshaft

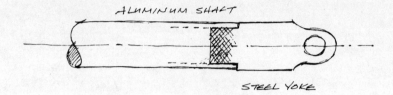

Figure 1   Aluminium driveshaft joined to the yoke by the Magnaform process

tube using the Magnaform process (see Figure 1). This process magnetically collapses a ring that forces the driveshaft tube into the spline of the yoke. Magnaforming is used, for example, to place the metallic end on an incandescent light bulb.

This was the first time that Magnaforming had been used at these power levels, and in the plant the equipment had a high downtime experience. To minimize this problem the plant tended to operate the equipment at the lowest possible power level. This action accelerated a longer-term problem which would have appeared anyway because of the natural compliance of this mechanical joint. A clicking sound that occurred as the driver changed gears was eventually produced because the joint loosened over time when the yoke and tube moved relative to each other due to changing torques. Although the driveshaft was fully safe and capable of transferring all torque requirements, the clicking sound became an annoyance to the driver and clearly a high warranty problem without a cure.

It was decided by several engineers that the driveshaft should be made using a fully connected weld joint. But the Sterling plant had no experience in welding aluminium. They were also quite frankly told the problem had to be solved and that if they could not weld this joint the job would have to be moved to an outside source with the loss of over 300 jobs at the plant. Obviously the plant floor people wanted a solution.

Powertrain Engineering contacted me (Al Oros) for help because of work I had done for them on welding of experimental aluminum axles. MDC committed to taking responsibility for developing a welding procedure for manufacturing the aluminum driveshaft. Since this product was in production and no fix was then available for the noise problem, it was imperative that the change in manufacturing processes be made as quickly as possible. This eliminated laser, electron beam, or friction welding processes which would require long development times. Since the plant was already using GMAW (gas-metal-arc-welding) for joining steel driveshafts, we decided (Oros, his co-worker Sawyer and other associates at MDC including the managers who agreed) to pursue this process.

Development

A DOE (design of experiment) was established to quantify the effect of welding factors on the weld that was produced. Factors investigated were: current, voltage, travel speed, torch position, torch incident angle, torch tip to work distance, wire type, and shielding gas.

Generally, only inert gases are used when welding aluminum. However, in this case since this would be a single-pass weld and since the highest possible travel speed was needed, it was decided that an argon/oxygen gas mixture should be used as one of the shielding gases. This is against common practice; usually great care is taken to avoid oxygen. Oxygen increases the electron emissivity of the metal surface by increasing the amount of oxide on the surface and affects the arcing process usually to its detriment. However, we reasoned that the action of the oxygen would stabilize the arc and allow faster welding speeds. Since a second weld was not to be placed on the joint, the increased oxide on the surface of the weld would not interfere with the strength of the weld.

From the DOE the correct level of each welding factor was chosen so that the most robust process possible would be produced. We found that the weld penetration produced when welding with these settings was within 20 thousandths of an inch of that predicted by the DOE. After our preliminary work we involved the Sterling engineers more closely and two hundred aluminum driveshafts were produced and tested using the procedure established by the DOE. These driveshafts passed all fatigue and static torque load requirements and it was decided to produce 2,000 driveshafts to test the consistency of the process. This test, using more Sterling personnel, was also successful.

As a final proof and to be able to transfer this knowledge to the plant, it was decided to pilot the process at MDC using Sterling plant personnel. The exact welding equipment that would be used in production was designed, built and fitted to temporary fixturing and 20,000 driveshafts were welded on our plant floor. This pilot was a key to the success of this project.

Fred Sawyer, who was my right-hand man through all this, and I then gave assistance to the equipment manufacturer and worked in the Sterling plant when installing the production equipment on the plant floor.

Comments

The project was driven by the determination (and for the plant people, the desperation) of Ford's Transmission and Chassis Division (T&C) to solve this warranty problem without having to take the work from the Sterling plant. As the project progressed, reports had to be made to T&C top management, and eventually a final summary to the executive vice president. The work was notable because it was a swiftly created solution with remarkably widespread cooperation prompted by the mastery displayed by Oros and Sawyer and their practiced willingness to share with others.

The success of this project was dependent upon the systematic approach that was used, particularly the statistical DOE employed to establish the welding process. As an example, the DOE showed that torch position was second only to welding current in importance to the robustness of the process. Because of this, unlike all GMAW equipment supplied to the plant in the past, this equipment was built so that the torch position could not be adjusted.

Oros insisted that none of the factor levels established by the DOE be changed without running another DOE to identify the effect of any such change. When a minor problem was encountered during installation of the equipment on the plant floor, the first thing that the welding equipment manufacturer wanted to do was to adjust the welding parameters. Oros protested this vigorously and the plant supported his position. It was later found that the source of the problem was an electrical short in the equipment that was cured by isolating the welding wire from ground. When these minor equipment problems were addressed, this was said to be the smoothest implementation of a new process ever experienced by the Sterling plant. The plant had Oros present the work of the whole team as a part of the presentation they gave to win the Ford Q-1 award (a prestigious quality award).

A second part of this project which had great importance was having personnel from the plant run the pilot at MDC. Because of this, when the project moved to the Sterling plant, it didn't just involve an "expert" handing off some technology to the plant, this was a technology that the plant personnel had "bought-into" because they had been a part of the development of that technology. In the beginning,

Fred Sawyer and Al Oros watched over the pilot closely. In the last weeks of the pilot they checked far more infrequently, perhaps once a day to see how things were going but they really were no longer needed to make the process run smoothly. This manufacturing development project was a landmark.

Summary

- **There was a real problem**, recognized both by a plant management and by plant floor people.
- **Oros' team** and he himself were **known by the people who had the problem**. If they didn't recognize Al Oros as an expert before all this work, they surely did afterwards.
- **Al Oros and Fred Sawyer are experts**. They quickly eliminated processes that didn't make sense (too long development times, cost, complexity, etc.) Only experts can make these decisions and be prepared to live with them . . . both parts being important.
- **They invented something new**. Radical. Their reasoning was based on experience, need, and intuition.
- **They used the right (accepted) methods**: design-of-experiments procedures. Start small and build up to a level that will provide compelling evidence. Form a team; build in your customers. Do a pilot and move with the results to make the sure thing happen in the plant that happened in the piloting area.
- **They gave as much credit as possible to the plant**.
- **They exited gracefully** and didn't wait for the applause.

Notice that Al and Fred didn't spend years on this project. The plant didn't have years to wait for a solution (they were dying), and so whatever invention could be involved had to be based on what they already knew and what they could reason out in the hours of "discussion work" they had with other peers at MDC. So I must add one coda.

- **It helps to be lucky.** I do notice, however, that the only "lucky" development engineers are ones who have already scored a few successes.

Ideally, I would like to describe all the successes that I saw created by the people I worked with. But it would become repetitious and probably tedious to read all the stories. This is a problem for me because I like all the stories and especially all the people. In order to narrow my choices, the particular case illustrations have been chosen as extremes. The first example described was one of quick hard work and success. The second to be described had ups and downs all along the way, even though it also proved successful in the long run and also became a landmark. It involved several engineers who contributed to a change at Ford's Dearborn Tool and Die plant. The description of the challenge and the events written by Joe Walacavage for my use here is also given more or less in his words.

The phone call

The Dearborn Tool & Die (DT&D) project was initiated in October 1987, with a Saturday phone call from the assistant general manager of Body and Assembly Operations, to Chuck

Feltner, who was then our manager at the Manufacturing Development Center (MDC). Mr Feltner's Operations Engineering (OE) group had recently completed a systems analysis study of the Ford St Louis plant at his request. The study used *discrete event simulation* (a computer-based visualization of what is going on) to assist in identifying the key bottleneck areas in the plant which were limiting Aerostar production to well below the planned launch volumes.

We had some success in helping St Louis, so this assistant general manager was now requesting that the OE group take an overall look at the process of building stamping dies within Ford to determine opportunities for reducing the time to complete an entire die-build program. The building of dies is on the critical path of the corporate new car program time line (now called World Class Timing). A typical die-build program currently takes about 14–17 months to complete (1987).

First steps

The first step for OE was to get a feel for the size of the process and problem. Initial work was performed by Dan Piercecchi, one of our engineers, and Gene Coffman, our group leader, which involved doing a high-level statistical study that looked at historical timing records from die design through die construction and die tryout. From this effort it was concluded that a more detailed model was required which could mimic the interactions and material flow within the DT&D plant before any meaningful questions could be answered. The modeling technology chosen for use was discrete event simulation, specifically the SIMAN language, because of its flexibility in modeling applications and OE's good track record in using it.

Customer versus problem owner

It's a bad start to be from a corporate staff, show up in a plant where everyone is already busting their butts (i.e. working extremely hard) and tell them that while you know little about their business, you are there to help them anyway. Hopefully in these situations there is someone of significant rank among senior plant management who initiates the requests for outside Division help. In this case, it was the DT&D plant manager's boss's boss's boss who said that the plant needed our help. Not exactly an initial close link here to the problem holder. Having a customer who is not the direct owner of "the problem" made for some slow going early on in the project. As the project and modeling effort matured and DT&D saw that we (OE–MDC) were not out to "get them", DT&D gradually evolved into being the customer. DT&D management began asking their own questions to the models. DT&D eventually used model results and OE recommendations as part of their future facility expansion project justification package, and the whole project succeeded. I'll discuss in more detail what I consider to be the positive turning point for the project.

General Patton

Before any type of simulation effort can get off the ground, one must first develop a good understanding of the problem. For this project, finding out how dies are built at DT&D turned out to be a non-trivial task. We went down to the DT&D Tool Coordination office and asked for some process sheets which would give us an idea of the processing sequences required to build dies. Of course, no such animal existed. There was a lot of localized expertise at DT&D. For instance, the Kellering (machining) supervisor could swamp you with all kinds of detail regarding his domain, but had little to offer in explaining interactions within other areas of the plant.

A little luck never hurts. We were very fortunate early in the project to be able to hire as a consultant the retired ex-production manager from DT&D, Don Patton. General Patton, as he was called by some of his former people from the plant, had over 35 years of experience in building dies at DT&D, but had very little (less than zero) knowledge of computer-driven manufacturing simulation. Our goal was to use Don to assist us in mapping out how all the castings used to make dies at DT&D flowed through various machining and handwork processes until a functioning die was built.

Don is a very nice person. Don at that time was a chain cigarette smoker. Don is a straight shooter. Don was used to communicating with (mostly ordering) people who understood the die-building business. Don had little patience. OE's Dan Piercecchi was a "silver fox" type with over 35 years of experience in various areas of Ford. Dan is a very nice person also. Dan is a pipe smoker. Dan was a local head-figure with the Republican party (so he knew how to work people to get a "yes" vote). Dan was a very patient person.

Dan's job was to work with General Don in mapping out how DT&D works, in modeling terms. It was a love–hate type of arrangement. Don started off by stating that there was no way to map the plant since no two dies were alike. Dan would not accept this answer. Don was not used to having his judgments questioned like this and would readily voice his counter point in a loud fashion. Dan would say the right things to calm the General down, and then proceed to analyze the situation again. A typical disagreement between the two would consist of them exchanging their opinions with increasing volume, followed by a smoke cloud rising out of Dan's corner office area (Ford still allowed smoking in office areas at this time) with the combined stench of Camel cigarettes and the aroma of pipe tobacco. At times I thought they were passing a peace pipe back and forth to make up after a yelling session. There were instances where Don would get so upset that he'd vocally storm out of the room into the aisle to have a cigarette by himself. He would then return to Dan's desk and the two of them would talk about old cars, Ford stock, and grandchildren like nothing had ever happened.

The persistence of Dan with Don paid off. The work with Don really accelerated once we had some basic die processing information broken down and put into a graphical model where the General could see how we were using his information to simulate casting movement at DT&D. Once Don started to understand the modeling world, he started describing the workings of the plant in modeling terms, so we had to create fewer logic conversions. Don started watching the model daily to make sure we had all of his knowledge in it, and he even started coming to work in the morning with an addition/change list for the model already made up. Now we couldn't shut the guy up. Don really got wrapped up in this PacMan thing, as he called it. (PacMan was an early computer screen game.) He even showed up on his own time, unannounced (and uninvited), to a study review meeting with the plant manager, and also to a higher level review meeting where he freely spoke about how great this modeling stuff was. He was a great asset to us, thanks to the man himself and also to Dan's work.

Some progress

After two months of working with Don to document the die building process, the team determined that dies followed one of nine generic flow-of-work paths through DT&D, where each path describes the routing and "baseline" processing times of all the castings required to build that type of die (i.e. draw die outer, flange die outer, pierce die, draw die inner, cut-off die, etc.). Once these flow-of-work paths were defined, models could then be designed to simulate the overall procedure by classifying a die as one of the nine generic dies, assigning a start-work date (castings arrival into DT&D), and applying a weighted processing time factor. The weighted time factor was applied to the "baseline" processing times to account for different die sizes and complexities. We took the flow-of-work paths documentation down to DT&D and asked the present die construction supervisors to review them. We received extremely positive feedback. In fact, they asked for copies as they had never seen this type of documentation which described the interactions of their areas.

Bad boys

Validating the models was a reiterative process that allowed us to get our hands slapped by DT&D a couple of times early in the project. The approach used to validate the models was to use actual historical data from various die-build programs as input to the model, run the models, and then compare actual die-build program completion dates with model predicted completion dates. Early test runs had the model completing build programs 3–4 months faster than actual records indicated. Well, that meant that the model was missing a restricting resource somewhere. Because we still didn't really know what we were doing, we made some poor assumptions, thought we had the answers, and presented results at a meeting with the DT&D plant manager.

Throughout the course of the project, the plant manager had shown extreme patience with us "seagulls" from Staff as he once called us. He would always make room on his busy calendar for us, allow us to finish our sentences and explain all our nice graphs and charts, and listen intently to our conclusions. He would not debate for debate's sake, or ask meaningless questions just because a person of his rank is supposed to ask questions. Also, he would not keep secrets if he disagreed with findings or conclusions, and this became especially obvious during our meeting. When we outsiders told him that by better manning in his plant he could instantly reduce program build time by two months . . . well, let's just say I was glad that I had numbered all my feathers beforehand so I knew where they belonged after they all got blown off. One engineer from Tool Coordination got fired three times during the meeting for supposedly not having enough people on the floor.

To cut a long story down, a few things were learned: one, don't try and simulate what you think people do unless you absolutely have to; two, don't believe manpower data unless you are the one generating it; three, it's better to be approximately correct than precisely inaccurate; and four, never sit next to a plant manager when presenting precisely inaccurate results.

Doing better

The OE team did eventually get the models validated, with simulated program completion times falling within 5 percent of actual times. As it turned out, we even earned a few brownie points from the plant manager by telling his boss that the work by DT&D two years earlier to enlarge a particular area of floor space had reduced program build time by a month.

Good boys

With validated models, the team now set off on a traditional simulation study in trying to identify and quantify the effect of bottleneck resources within DT&D ... and what we found agreed with DT&D's gut feelings. More brownie points. Then, when we used the model to quantify "time-wise" the impact of lacking sufficient resources we started getting phone calls from DT&D requesting additional model runs with different conditions – a change from the team always contacting them. More brownie points. When model results identified the major bottleneck area, and specifically pointed to actions that would lift the limiting resource, DT&D became both our partner and our customer. We were now working for DT&D. There was no memo or reorganization letter that said this, but there was a change in attitude. OE had always been treated fairly by DT&D, but early on, one had the feeling that DT&D didn't mind seeing this group from the Manufacturing Development Center leave their building at the end of a meeting. Now, DT&D was even asking if we could come to high-level review meetings on their behalf, not because the high-level managers had requested us.

From the bottom up

A rather interesting day needs to be mentioned here before I leave Tryout (an early stage in the plant's process). I went into DT&D one morning to review what we called the "clean sheet" model results with a key engineer. I was using a single piece of paper that had series of data matrixes which showed how sensitive simulated program completion time was particular to presses used in the model. This document was simply an output from the model and was not meant for any type of formal presentation (there was even a coffee cup ring on it). The engineer was impressed with the findings, we shook hands, and I returned to MDC. Later that morning I got a call from the plant manager asking me to come back to DT&D right away to further explain the one-page report I had left. Obviously the engineer had pushed the document up to his office. I asked Gene Coffman to accompany me back down to DT&D (we were both numbering our feathers again as we were driving down the Southfield freeway). We explained the findings to the plant manager. He was impressed, we shook hands, and Gene and I returned to MDC with feathers intact. Around lunchtime that same day I got another call from the plant manager requesting that Gene and I meet him at his boss's office in one hour to again explain the one-pager. After reviewing the "clean sheet" results with this more senior gentleman, it was suggested that the one-pager be forwarded and explained to his boss.

So, later that same afternoon, the plant manager, Gene and I met with his boss and again explained the one-pager. Two days later, all of us including Gene, and you-know-who (me) had a meeting with the next higher level to explain the you-know-what (the report). The summary message of the you-know-what was ammunition for an intended action by our new teammate – the plant manager – and quite important to him in that it provided hard numbers to support his view, rather than being a subjective argumentative reply. At this point in the project, DT&D not only was the customer, but also now owned the models.

Comments

There were many other stories in Joe Walacavage's complete account of the development work, all of them written with the humor of hindsight and not the terror of the moment.

My comments are arranged for comparison with those about Al Oros' project. At the start of all this work:

- **There was no problem clearly recognized by plant floor people**, even if an upper-upper part of management saw needs.
- **The OE team was not known to the plant** at the start.
- **The OE team did not know anything about the tool and die business**.
- Although there eventually was **invention, it was not a clear single item**, but part of the expertise and experience base of the OE team . . . analysis and model building was what they did best.
- **There were no accepted or right methods** like the DOE used by Oros.
- **They didn't give credit to the plant and they didn't exit gracefully** . . . in fact, they had a tough time being allowed to stay in the plant. Much later they were successful and worked as part of the DT&D team. Today, they also appear to be "lucky".

These observations of conditions at the start of all this work negate those from the first description, one-by-one. The keys to success in the long run were the transformation of "who" wanted help from a "who" being the assistant general manager to "who" being the plant people; investing and spending the time for the operations engineering team to learn about the tool and die business; making the team known on the plant floor; making the OE's work clear to the plant people and showing the invention that had to be involved; and finally a non-interfering management attitude both from the assistant general manager and from the higher-level supervision at MDC.

A third example is given for another project in the Appendix to this book to show that projects which aren't at either extreme also follow the same path to success. It is more-or-less midway in terms of these needs for success which are in fact part of the prescription for "how to" in the art of manufacturing development.

You certainly need:

- plant people to positively want new technology, which comes easiest when there is a real problem;
- to be known to the plant people; and
- to be expert.

Generally you also need:

- enough change to make a difference (not trouble-shooting) . . . an invention;
- a pilot involving plant people where the right methods are used and are accepted;
- to give as much credit to the plant as possible;

- to exit gracefully and not applaud yourself – others will applaud you if there is success; and
- to be lucky.

The OE team at Dearborn Tool & Die started at the toughest extreme from Oros' team. Even though there was a plant problem, the plant didn't recognize it. The team had to create a situation where the plant people became believers, and did really want new technology. Of course, the OE team were experts in their own field to start with. What they didn't start with was knowledge about what the plant did and about "life" on the plant floor. Joe Walacavage and others had to spend hundreds of hours there; and Don Patton, a deeply knowledgeable man, became an OE team member. People moved; people became involved; credit was given to the plant and the plant people; there was close involvement of plant people and development people.

One of the things in this prescription I haven't discussed is the need "to be lucky". It is important, but let me leave it unexplained for now.

The new idea and the new technology

The first example here is described by Dave Courtney, the responsible engineer who started this project in July 1986 and persevered to be successful in developing and implementing Lightweight Sealers. Before a car is fitted out with its insides (trim) and with much of its functional parts (engine; chassis) and before it is painted, it is a body-in-white.

Sealers are used to cover and close-off (seal) the fitted edges of sheet metal which have been welded together to form the body-in-white. Sealers create an isolated interior that will be water-tight and they contribute somewhat to noise reduction.

Dave is knowledgeable about sealers. He knows the material suppliers; he knows the equipment suppliers (sealers are generally sprayed on); he knows the people in the plant and the body and assembly engineers who are responsible for specifications and processes. Again, I will use the successful engineer's words; I will use Dave's words.

Background

The lightweight sealers concept was born quite by accident during a visit to the Nordson Corporation in Amherst, Ohio. While discussing a totally unrelated subject, Nordson casually showed me a piece of "foamed" sealer material they had been experimenting with . . . not a sealer that could be applied to an automobile and not the same type of material . . . but wheels and gears began to whirr in my head and I thought, "I wonder if we could apply this technology to the pounds and pounds of sealer materials that we put into vehicle bodies". (Sealers preclude the intrusion of dust, water and noise into the passenger compartment.) Foaming these sealer materials would have the potential of saving both vehicle weight and total cost. We (Ford and Nordson) agreed that it might be beneficial to both of us, so the project was initiated.

The technology as now developed embodies an electromechanical device which the Nordson Corporation has named "FoamMix^{TM}". This device reduces the weight of these sealers by dissolving a gas (i.e. air or nitrogen) in the sealer material with a low-shear mixture under medium pressure. When this gas/ sealer solution is released to atmospheric pressure (during the application process), a uniform mixture of finely dispersed gas bubbles is produced (see Figure 2) which has the consistency of a closed cell "foam". With this concept, as expected, not only weight, but sealer expenditures are reduced.

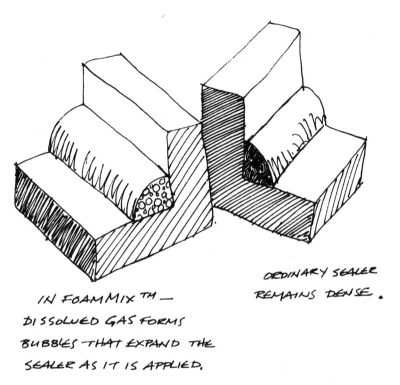

IN FOAMMIX ™ —
DISSOLVED GAS FORMS
BUBBLES THAT EXPAND THE
SEALER AS IT IS APPLIED.

ORDINARY SEALER
REMAINS DENSE.

Figure 2 Foamed sealer application using the electro-mechanical
FoamMix™ process

Development

Our Body Shell Sealing Department of the Body Engineering
Office has responsibility for specifying which materials are
applied to vehicle bodies. Early on I had discussions with these
people as to the potential benefits of the FoamMix™ technology
and its positive impact on Corporate Average Fuel Economy
(CAFE) standards.

However, the idea bounced around for some time because the
"CAFE" problem, although real, was "Corporate". The biggest

"shot in the arm" for the project came from an engineer who was the weight analyst for the Tempo/Topaz vehicle line. He had a task (i.e. a problem or a need) to remove weight from this line of vehicles so that Ford could offer a V-6 engine as an option to our customers. We tested the FoamMix^{TM} concept on the interior floor pan seams, where the bulk of the sealers are applied, and it proved successful (i.e. an in-house pilot was run). The weight savings generated with the FoamMix^{TM} process, coupled with other weight saving projects, allowed this option to become a reality.

This became one of the easier projects (I've seen) to implement into production. Early on, our customer, the engineers (Body Shell Sealing of the Body Engineering Office), were pushing to get it implemented as soon as possible. Their push was the best driver in turn to push the ultimate user, Body and Assembly Operations, to want the technology.

There was still a lot of work. Not only did we have to satisfy the existing material performance specifications of the Body Engineering Office, but we also had to satisfy the minimum equipment standards of the Body and Assembly Operations before we could even place a piece of the FoamMix^{TM} equipment in one of our assembly plants for a trial. This took many months of testing, but we were successful.

A certain amount of salesmanship was also still involved in gaining acceptance for this project. Many presentations had to be made to various engineering activities, conferences and forums to educate people to the benefits of this technology. I made videotapes of the process in action to make the selling easier. These were sent to various assembly plants interested in the FoamMix^{TM} process.

Comments

Eventually two pilots were run, one of 5,000 vehicles in one plant and one of over 23,000 vehicles of another car line in a different plant. As a result of these and the successful ground work, the process was fully implemented into production in the autumn of 1991 on an appropriate car line and will spread over time to most Ford vehicles and operations. Dave Courtney is still responsible (at the time of writing) for testing to prove the process in Europe and acts as a consultant to all plants.

Let us analyze Dave's words. He had a new idea. He worked on it with increasing self-interest until he found a customer. Then he and this first-stage customer (not in the plant but someone with a need) spent a lot of time and effort turning the ultimate-users into customers so that they became people who would really want the technology.

It helped that Dave was known in the plants where pilots were run; and it helped that Dave was an expert. It should be clear that Dave Courtney really did just the same things that Al Oros and Fred Sawyer did and what Joe Walacavage and his team did, with one very important extra. He had to find a customer – each new idea requires finding a customer. If you proceed without one, chances are that you will fail.

This challenge to find a customer has to be added to the prescription for success in manufacturing development. Then, if a *new idea* must somehow be transformed into solving a plant problem, what about the next more complex category in development, the *new technology*.

Very simply I contend that you cannot implement new technologies as such.

Here is where managers and management can be of value. Managers hire people. Managers should contribute to strategic decisions and should know about technologies that are developing outside; about technologies that are needed by their customers; and about technologies that their customers don't know about, but would find useful if they did when the technologies were ripe. Why else should managers be used and paid? Further than this, managers working with their people and their customers should (must) focus specifically on that *one special new idea* in a new technology *that will solve a plant problem (challenge)*. My example in this area of new technology comes from powder metallurgy and powder metal forming.

By 1969 Ford, GM and Chrysler had each separately started research and development programs in a growing new technology which consisted of fabricating automotive components close to the final shape desired by forging powder metal preforms. The new process consisted of making a powdered metal part close to the final component shape (by powder metallurgy) and then forging it to eliminate porosity (powder metal forming) achieving mechanical properties equal to or greater than those of the originally dense metal.

One key to achieving superior mechanical properties for critically stressed parts was working with clean powder. This required a good knowledge base in the technologies of powder metallurgy and knowing who was capable in these areas. Early on, Ford formed a close working relationship with suppliers to assure cleanliness of powders. A second key was good design related to meeting the working stresses a part would see. This required a good knowledge of the forming process, and what it would produce, and the ability to interest product designers. Here is where the story, adapted from words written by Stan Mocarski, starts:

Connecting rods

Connecting rods were quickly identified in the early years by the managers as components likely to benefit from this new technology. By 1972 the feasibility of using powder metal rods had been established in the laboratory through bench fatigue, dynamometer, and vehicle durability testing. The new technology, however, was not endorsed by the traditional powertrain component engineers. Fully accounted cost savings were not foreseen and the piece price was a penalty compared with the traditional forged connecting rod shown in the blank form in Figure 3.

Time passed and the managers did not get their job done. They didn't know enough to fully specify the benefits of the new idea and they didn't help make real customers because they didn't have real benefits to describe.

By 1981 Toyota in Japan who had seen the potential, both in their own research work and in that freely published by other companies, had won the race. They began using powder metal connecting rods in some engines. Meanwhile, work in the United States had led to application of the process to other parts at various companies, but to none which might be regarded as critical.

A connecting rod in an engine is critical – if one breaks most of an engine can be destroyed and most likely the manufacturers as well, since by the 1980s few engines "threw rods", a phrase from the 1930s. Managers of the technologies were apparently unsure about the new process and the research and development work slowed down except for a few fanatics. I, Stan Mocarski, was one; I wouldn't give up; just as importantly, my managers let me go on.

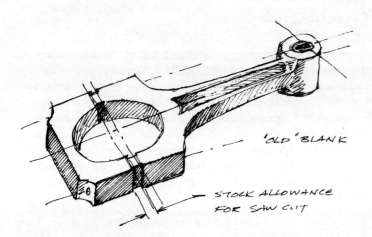

Figure 3 An original connecting rod

Several times I almost generated enough interest in programs but there was never a clear company customer. If the product engineer wanted the program, the manufacturing engineer in the plant was stymied by investment barriers (real, not imagined ones), and vice-versa. Then came another chapter. By continuing to be a lobbyist for the virtues of powder metal technology for engine components, our team at MDC in 1982/83 was requested to develop a powdered metal (p/m) forged connecting rod for a new 1987 engine by Engine Engineering. Although the request was made at a high level, all the engineers, up and down the organization knew us because we had persevered in meeting and persuading them all. (By the way, a 1987 engine starts to be built early in 1986.)

Under a tight timing schedule, over 1,000 parts were forged at MDC to support preproduction engine build and for establishing machining parameters by production machine tool builders. By being able to tailor the alloys, the p/m material developed had 250 percent better machinability characteristics than conventional steel while maintaining the superior mechanical properties.

Then came a real problem, but since we had seen it before (we had not only become reasonable experts in powder metallurgy, but in getting things done), we were determined to succeed and we were prepared. A particular parts plant was initially considered as a production site, but because of the critical process controls required and the limited payback (i.e. the investment problem), this parts plant refused to invest in the new technology. However, being prepared, we worked with Purchasing to select an outside supplier. Although the supplier had to catch up with the developments while starting production, they had some lead time because this was a possible step we had foreseen. At the same time MDC was testing and revalidating the new supplier's parts. An extensive effort was required just to develop a non-destructive test method to help overcome initial production difficulties (many months).

Towards the key date things seemed to be in hand. All along, both Engine Engineering and Engine Division (the manufacturing people who would assemble the supplier's rods into the engine) had a fallback program – the standard forged steel connecting rod, both tried and true. That they wanted the new rod at all was a miracle. MDC's "sales people" (the whole structure, our team, the managers) promised the potential of better control (i.e. better assembly quality), eventually lower weight rods (better engine quality), and other potentials. But at the outset the rods had to be designed better, stronger, etc. . . . "just in case" . . . so all we had was potential.

Then, just as initial production was to begin, a machinability problem was encountered at the engine plant. MDC identified the problem as hard particles in the raw powder. The powder material supplier could not resolve this problem in time for production. Again, we and Purchasing were prepared: the problem was solved and the program was saved by flying the powder in from an overseas supplier.

The program was saved because of established credibility with all the engine people, and having the whole of MDC behind us as a much larger team. This last problem appeared on a Thursday in early 1985 and the solution was guessed on the Friday which happened to be the deadline for the fallback program. MDC offered up all its staff to work all weekend to prove the solution or surrender by 9:00 a.m. Tuesday at the latest. It was proved in time and the program was still on "go". Curiously all the engine people, from the involved chief engineer downwards, were even more reassured after this massive people effort.

The new rod was launched with the new engine but in all of this, the idea of an "involved plant" was really two plants. Not just the engine plant but the supplier plant as well. The supplier was excellent but the technology was not easily transferred to the supplier. Early manufacturing difficulties continued. These had to be overcome by quick diagnosis of the problems after metallurgical examination by MDC and quick responsive action by the supplier. Continual monitoring of the parts by fatigue testing and metallurgical analysis resulted in an upgrading of the properties of the part and raised confidences in the process.

Comments

Eventually all of this enabled the next generation of connecting rods for a new engine to be even lighter in weight with a greater safety factor. It also contributed to less shaking force and a quieter, better engine.

Stan Mocarski along with Peter Hoag, David Yeager and Dao-Liang Wu of various Engine operations received the 1986 Henry Ford Technological Award "for development and production implementation of powder metal connecting rods".

Now the story goes on from here with a second new idea and a second success. But this time Mocarski was an expert from the start and was believed in mostly and most importantly by the Engine people, who were confirmed customers.

Fracture splitting of powder metal connecting rods

Regular review of competitive and other industry components often pays large dividends. During one of these reviews it was noted that an outboard engine connecting rod which operates under much smaller loads was forged with an integral cap and fracture split to separate the cap from the rod (see Figure 4). Other small engines also used this idea. The rough fractured surface becomes a mating surface between the cap and the rod which does not allow any cap shift in the direction perpendicular to the axis of the rod. This is a considerable advantage because cutting and grinding of the mating surfaces is eliminated as well as a significantly more expensive fastening system which requires, in effect, a doweling of the two parts at assembly.

In 1985 while the powder metal rod was on its way a renewed development team consisting of personnel from MDC, Engine Design and Manufacturing Engineering was created to apply this next technological step to a second new engine, the 4.6L modular which was to be built at a new engine plant. In this case the process had to be proven capable for production even earlier to be in time for purchase of rod splitting equipment.

The first generation fracturing fixture was built and the first rods were split using liquid nitrogen to embrittle the material and promote a clean fracture. Immediately MDC started bench

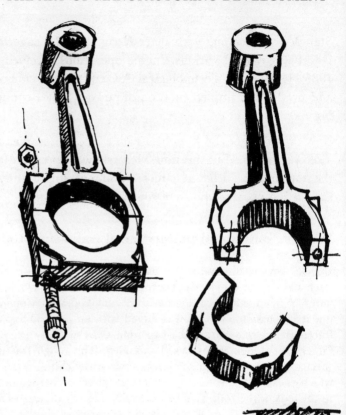

IRREGULARITIES
OF THE FRACTURED
FACES "LOCK" TOGETHER,
PERMITTING THE ELIMINATION
OF THRU HOLE, LONG SCREW
AND NUT — REPLACED BY A
SHORTER SELF-TAPPING SCREW.

Figure 4   Engine connecting rod with integral cap fracture split
to separate the cap from the rod

testing of the rods for fatigue life; and feasibility was established. Development continued on the splitting operation. Type, size, and shape of the notch as well as designs of the splitting mechanism were investigated. A refined second generation fixture allowed better splitting and showed that the splitting operation could be formed at room temperature. Several methods of splitting were evaluated for production.

Enough confidence was established to allow MDC to pass the final fixture on to Engine Division (ED) in early 1988. Working with the machine tool designers, ED was able to further refine the process and to develop a machine which could split connecting rods during a cycle of 4.5 seconds. Two of these machines were installed at the Romeo engine plant.

Romeo was a refurbished tractor plant dedicated to improving engine manufacturing for a "modular" family of engines. One of the production concepts used to promote worker involvement was establishment of job-specific teams. The team that was responsible for the connecting rod splitting operation named themselves the "Rod Busters" which they had emblazoned on their shirts. As you might expect, by the time they were in operation, they didn't know about me (Mocarski) or about MDC's role in developing the process. They didn't have to know – they now owned the process; it was theirs.

One great advantage of the rod splitting is that it provides an additional quality check for every rod produced. Several manufacturing improvements at the rod supplier were able to be addressed through detective work that was initiated by abnormalities found during the cracking operation. At the time of this writing many millions of rods have been successfully split and are running in Ford engines.

Comments

The method has proved successful and exhibits an overall cost advantage with fewer parts required for assembly and lower capital costs required. Also, the optimally engineered design provides a low reciprocating weight resulting in a more reliable, quieter engine at less cost. In consequence, several new engines which will be introduced by 1996 are being designed with powder metal fracture split connecting rods.

Notice the briefer story. With Mocarski as a recognized expert and confirmed customers who knew him and his team, the process of recognizing and enabling the application of a new idea was much easier.

The concept of a master

By now you must realize that I have a special regard for Al
Oros, Fred Sawyer, Joe Walacavage, Tony Mansour
(introduced in the Appendix), Dave Courteney, Stan
Mocarski and for dozens of others in their class. Well, who
are they? I implied earlier that I believe they are well
practiced Masters of the art of manufacturing development
and that they resemble the Zen Masters who study and
respect their own arts. I cannot prove this but I can argue
the case by comparing profiles of the two sets of Masters.

I personally have not studied as a pupil of Zen. My
recognition of Zen does, however, stretch back in time. A

good friend had offices in a public building where my Ford operation of that time was housed and we got to know each other. One interesting characteristic became apparent through increased contact, I learned that I could judge his business success by his moods. If he was serious, choppy, and preoccupied or dedicated, business was good; if he was light-hearted, soft, and ready to spend more time, business was bad.

We spoke about this observation and about how most people reacted differently to pressures, most often with stress or anxiety. Eventually we traded book titles and among the ones I gave him was *Zen in the Art of Archery* written by Eugen Herrigel sometime in the 1930s (the date is unclear). My friend was taken by the book. Eventually he sought a teacher and became a pupil of Zen for some years. His life changed but his attitude didn't. Earlier he had founded two engineering-related businesses which supported him and his life-style. Unfortunately these went into bankruptcy in one of our recessions. Everything went. He himself "changed into a pastry chef" after attending a school in Paris. Now he has a large successful pastry-and-dessert business in Chicago.

I doubt that my friend needed Zen to bounce back and be successful. He didn't spend his energies focusing on why he failed, he put his efforts into new projects that used his special skills and enjoyment of cooking, a love of learning new ways, and a sense of business. He didn't basically change; his style remained the same, but details of his life altered. I was amazed by his resilience in "making a living" and even more amazed by his style or his way of living, his attitudes and the way he tried to learn what his customers wanted – even if they didn't yet realize their wants.

We had also played tennis together. At that time there was a popular American book called *The Inner Game of Tennis* by W. Timothy Gallwey which suggests a focus on process not on inner self-judgment. Both the "inner game" and the Zen book stress practice and underline personal involvement.

Both books also encourage looking at what you do right and stress the act of repeating these right things when you find out what they are. They suggest the practice of success and not the examination of failure.

You see: I believe that it is quite proper for the production engineer, who is involved with keeping production going and not usually involved with new manufacturing development, to learn by his failure or for you to pursue any other kind of operation and learn by your failures. It is not good to learn tennis or right to do development that way. You learn from your successes.

The development men I mentioned at the start of this chapter told you about themselves when they wrote about what they did – not just the descriptions, but the words and the attitudes they convey. They focused on success, as did my friend.

Herrigel's book *Zen in the Art of Archery* is short, descriptive, and does not contain any prescriptions. He notes that Zen advocates the greatest economy of expression and that he had "found that what I cannot say quite simply and

without recourse to mystic jargon has not become sufficiently clear and concrete even to myself". There is no
mystic jargon in his book, but no prescription either. Yet in
spite of my background I was impressed enough to feel that
there had to be a way to create a prescription.

My background got in the way because I was trained as a
physicist and agree with the following quote from Lord
Kelvin: "When you can measure what you are speaking
about, and express it in numbers, you know something
about it . . . (otherwise) your knowledge is of a meager and
unsatisfactory kind; it may be the beginning of knowledge,
but you have scarcely in thought advanced to the stage of
science." Yet there are processes in my life which I don't
understand well and yet in which I operate well. I play
tennis and squash; I drive; I dance . . .

So in an attempt to create a prescription, here is a barest-of-
bare synopsis of the thoughts in *Zen in the Art of Archery*, a
book which was self-avowedly a synopsis of something that
cannot be synopsized:

- Zen and the "art" of anything is not concerned with
  bodily prowess or dexterity or taste, but with an ability
  "whose origin is to be sought in spiritual exercises and
  whose aim consists in hitting a spiritual goal". This
  implies *belief*, in whatever form you understand this
  word; and in other broader senses it implies that a
  Master of anything will always be a student of his art.
- There is almost no easily read Zen literature and Zen
  can only be understood by one who is in Zen. This

implies that you can only learn by doing and by doing in the company of others who also do this thing.

- Detachment, self-liberation, good education, passionate love for your chosen art, and veneration of teachers, are all hallmarks of the best students (and practitioners) of an art. This implies that you must have proper foundations and be suited to your job or you won't succeed.

- Do not grieve over bad shots and don't rejoice over good ones. This can be taken as: be realistic, choose the right targets and don't blame or credit yourself too much for failure or successes, especially when you deal with a process where you can't choose targets.

- You must be relaxed about what you do and you can only be relaxed if you are well practiced and know what you are doing. This seems obvious and means that you must concentrate on the way to success and concomitantly disregard any review of failures and how to "correct" them.

- To talk about your art (Zen) is almost betrayal. This implies that nothing becomes modesty better than silence. Accomplishments speak better for themselves than reports.

- Be prepared to spend years, and have the inner strength to persevere and enjoy them.

In other words:

1. have belief and remain a student.
2. learn by doing.

3. be suited to your task/choose tasks that suit you.
4. choose the right targets.
5. concentrate (practice) on the "way" to success.
6. let successes (accomplishments) speak for themselves.
7. have the inner strength to spend years.

These, to me, are the link between manufacturing development and Zen. Herrigel's book does frame a set of instructions. They are not direct and they are not easy, but they are instructions on how you must act to hit the targets of your art.

Long after Herrigel's book was published his wife Gustie Herrigel wrote one on *Zen in the Art of Flower Arrangement,* for she had studied with a Master in this art while living in Japan. This latter book is also a good read but does not lead you to any level where a prescription of instruction can be abstracted as her husband's book does. Other books about Zen and the Zen arts seem even less helpful. Perhaps this is understandable if you believe that you need to spend years since you won't capture any essence of many years in a book which can be read in a hundred minutes.

Finally, what about good manufacturing development? I believe this gets done by people who have followed instructions like the seven listed above, and the instructions therefore also become a prescription for recognizing who the people are. In my opinion a good manufacturing developer must fit this profile. If this is true it also suggests a way of leading others into the practice of what is intrinsically an art.

In the preface *art* was defined as the conscious use of a skill acquired by experience, study or observation combined with creative imagination. The practitioners of an art are those who should be studied or observed.

The first and the second prescriptions and another example

In the preceding chapters we first paid attention to "what" manufacturing development is by reviewing some descriptions about successful projects. The observations about what the Oros/Sawyer team did were supplemented by observing that you must have a customer and that you cannot apply new technologies, only new ideas. By adding the warning about finding a customer and by making one change to the last item, which in the following list will be explained immediately, the combination yields a "how-to". Therefore, for the first prescription, you need:

- to reduce new technologies to the level of one new idea;
- to find a customer;

- the plant people to positively want new technology (easiest if there is a plant problem);
- to be known to the plant people;
- to be expert;
- enough change to make a difference;
- a pilot involving plant people;
- to give credit to the plant;
- to exit gracefully; and
- to be "lucky" – to be a Master.

The words "find a customer", as deduced from the examples given, can mean years of perseverance; and the word "lucky" has a special use. It means you must be a Master; you must fit the profile of being a Master. I haven't seen successful developers other than those who follow a prescription to:

- have belief and remain students;
- learn by doing;
- choose tasks that suit them;
- choose the right targets;
- concentrate on success;
- let successes speak for themselves; and
- have the inner strength to spend years

I propose that these are seven characteristics – the second prescription – of individuals who appear to be "lucky" to other people who do not know that these individuals have these characteristics.

The preceding sentence may be difficult to read, but I believe it is true. How many times do we hear someone remark on the achievement of another by saying, "he was just lucky"?

If all of this (i.e. the two complete lists just presented) is added up and analyzed, you end up with: know your technology; know the plant; know how to deal with people; persevere; focus on success; be modest. In many ways the Master who knows and does these things serves the task he attempts more than the employer he works for.

♦ ♦

This analysis reduces the book, so far, to a few lines; in fact it ends up with an almost trivial result because it is so obvious. Yet it certainly isn't what you find in books on technological innovation. It is too vague. It is too ungraspable. It is Zen-like. Unfortunately, it is too real. These are more or less the same checkpoints to be used in discussing good tennis (see *The Inner Game of Tennis*) or good dedicated effort to achieve anything.

This kind of sorting out doesn't set out goals. It doesn't dictate management practices or performance reviews or comparative salaries or anything procedural.

I don't believe that Master developers should be either constrained (punished for failures) or rewarded for successes especially; they should not be rewarded for anything but good processes and hard work. A set of peers will be all that is needed to judge rewards. The successful ones know who they are. People eventually recognize the Masters of an art and more particularly Masters recognize Masters.

All of this presents a problem. If a parent organization wants to progress, it should want to engage in progressive change. A manufacturing organization should want the best practices leading to the highest quality and the lowest costs. This doesn't easily call for radical change or invention and thus plants and plant people should be cautious . . . should be progressive but conservative, and should have learned by practice (i.e. from failures). It seems then, that development of inventions should not be a job done inside the manufacturing organization itself. Development can be done outside and bought, adapted, from some other ideas, or invented by another part of the parent to the manufacturing organization. But there have to be "experts" around who know whether or not the ideas are real/good/important. This thought is well illustrated in the last full-length manufacturing development example to be presented here.

The words are unprompted ones from Gene Coffman who would probably not be one of the world's choices as a Zen Master. In fact, I am not sure he will be flattered by this description. But as you read about a story he was involved in, I'm sure you'll agree that he fits the profile of a Master of manufacturing development. Read his words on a High Option Content Report (HOCR).

Origin

The project began in late 1987 with a request by a line supervisor at the Norfolk Assembly Plant. The data-processing department at this plant had developed a way to print out a list of jobs that would significantly impact her area, but she had to send someone to the computer room to get the information. As a labor-savings project (save the time it takes to walk to the computer room and back about once an hour), a request was initiated to print the information at the assembly line. Because of MDC's previous experience with vehicle broadcast data, we were asked to evaluate the request and ultimately asked to develop a solution.

But this was only the "seed" for what evolved into an important story. Because of our experience in vehicle assembly and vehicle option complexity and our working relationships with other assembly plants, this basic idea was "opened up" and "broadened" to many applications across many plants.

Technology description

To describe the technology involved in the HOCR system, one must first understand the environment that the system is a part of. The system is primarily used in the final assembly areas of our vehicle assembly plants. In these areas, assembly line workers add all the interior and exterior trim and chassis components to a painted "shell" of a car body. The vast majority of operations are performed manually and require varying amounts of effort depending on the number and type of options ordered by the customer. A form is printed and attached to each vehicle describing, in single letter codes, the various options and parts that are to be added to the vehicle. A typical operator will perform the following sequence of steps:

- read the form to determine the work to be done and the materials and tools needed;
- obtain the material and tools from temporary storage areas along the workstation;
- perform the required work; and
- if time permits, inspect the work, then go to the next vehicle.

An operator will have 1–2 minutes to perform the required tasks.

If there is not enough time to complete the work before the vehicle leaves the workstation, the task(s) can be left incomplete and a repair operator must complete the work at a later time. Since some vehicles require more work time than others, if "too many" high-work-content vehicles are scheduled "too close" together, an operator will need help to complete the required tasks on all the vehicles. When there is some warning that such a condition will occur, the line supervisor can assign someone to help this operator for a short time, preventing the required tasks from being missed and showing up as repairs later on.

The HOCR system is a computer tool that captures the vehicle build information as it is printed and then provides a way for plant people to access that information and view ahead of time any potential problems. A secondary application is that once the build information is available, the material control personnel can use the information to provide the materials needed in a more timely and ordered manner.

Once the vehicle build information was collected and stored on a computer, many other opportunities were identified to improve both direct and indirect operations. For example, a method to selectively print only the information needed by a group of operators in a more ergonomic format was successfully piloted and implemented.

Customer buy-in

Customer buy-in is a key to the success of any development project. In this case, customer buy-in was earned by months of working with the actual users of the system and doing whatever it took to meet their needs. A key part of our success was that our name and phone number were continuously displayed on the computer screen as the software was running. A second key was that we were not part of the manufacturing plant/division itself and therefore not competing for rewards inside the system. In this way, with respect to the first key, when something went wrong or if the user had questions about the system, the user could call up the developer and usually get an immediate answer to his or her questions and most importantly, directly communicate the problems back to the people who could help him or her. With respect to the second key, there never was any reporting about anyone with a problem or any failing-to-understand.

Development issues

There are three ways that you can develop something new – buy it, adapt another idea, or invent your own. In general, we used a combination of all three to complete the project. Our tactic was first to try to buy what was needed. If that didn't work or wasn't available, we would try to adapt something already developed for another purpose. As a last resort, we would invent something new. For the most part, the entire project was an evolution of adapting and enhancing what we already had (with a few creative features thrown in). For example, the software to collect the vehicle data was adapted from some software we had written to collect data for simulation models of the final assembly lines.

This continuous evolutionary process allowed us to respond more quickly to customer requests, and as new ideas/applications were identified, they were more easily incorporated as part of the development process.

Personalities

A part of the development process of this project was the generalization of a basic idea into something that had much broader impact. This was accomplished because of the team that came together as a result of having this system at each plant.

In every plant, there was at least one person who we could talk to about how their plant could make use of any new developments or ideas. The typical way a new idea became a part of the system was to go through a process of "expansion" before being implemented. Usually an idea came from one of the users. Typically, there was something they wanted to do or some type of information they wanted to see. These requirements came to us either in the form of a question (e.g. "Can I do xxxx with the HOCR system?") or as a request (e.g. "I could really use xxxx from the system; this much is already there and could you add the rest?").

From these requests, we first discussed how we could accommodate the request, what the impact of the changes required to implement the request was likely to be, and how else this idea could be used. We would then select two or three other plants to discuss the ideas with before attempting to implement them. Often this would generate a response such as: "We don't have that problem, but here is a different way we could use the same idea." Also, any impact specific to a given plant that would make the change would be discussed to make sure that by making a change requested by one user there wouldn't be a consequent negative impact upon some other users.

Broadened/implementation

After installation of the first "prototype version" of the system at the first two plants, other plants heard about the HOCR system and wanted to become a part of it; and of course they each had their own ideas about how to make use of the system. One of our roles in the technology transfer was to help spread the ideas, and particularly those ideas about different ways of using the system from one plant to the next. At periodic "CIM Conferences", (CIM is computer-integrated manufacturing), we would give presentations on the latest changes to the system and share some of the ways other plants were using the system. This promoted a very open exchange of ideas between plants so that the system appeared to "spread out into the plants on its own".

Keys to success

- Background of the development team (primarily two people, Jim McAlpine and me, imbedded in a group of six or seven people) with respect to the environment in which the system was to be used.
- Anticipation/understanding by the development team of what the customers really wanted when requests were made. Many requests were accommodated with "The system can already do that, just change these parameters to . . .".
- The ability to generalize basic concepts into broader applications and to incorporate them into the system in the most general form possible.
- Putting the name and phone number of someone from the development team on the screens and responding to requests.
- Not being a competitor to the active people in the plants.
- The fostering of a user community and making them a part of the team. Using their ideas to improve the system and acknowledging their contributions.

Comments

These closing words of the unprompted description by Gene Coffman emphasize all of the overriding keys for the Master. Be an expert (know your technology). Know the plant. Choose the right targets. Concentrate on success. Perhaps it is also appropriate for me to add a few words dealing with attitude:

- A successful leader in this art never literally leads – he follows (e.g. the process of learning transfer that went from plant to plant).

- Those who cannot feel the littleness of great things in themselves are apt to overlook the greatness of little things in others (e.g. the many small requests accommodated by this team which led to a steadily improving, widespread and successful process).
- Truth can often be reached only through the comprehension of opposites (consider the simple task at hand – to give the proper information to the right people at the right time – and the massively complex tool used to complete the task – a computer was used to solve this problem).

Finally, let me emphasize strongly the Master's combination of understanding the people in the plant and understanding the computer, by noting a Zen observation:

A man with a lighted lantern went searching for fire to cook his supper. Had he known what fire was, he would have satisfied his hunger sooner.

The vision of new technology and the third prescription

The chapter about the "new idea" and the "new technology" was dissatisfying with respect to new technology. It was just briefly mentioned as a source activity for the "new idea", while noting that managers as well as masters contribute to choosing new technology. There isn't very much more to say unless you are writing a book on technology management, and yet, some of that is needed here because it is part of manufacturing development.

So far we have described some aspects of manufacturing development and have established two prescriptions, one for "how to" and one for "who". Now we will try for a third prescription which deals with the management of manufacturing development and therefore adds to the description of what it is.

Someone has to decide which Masters are to be hired or developed. This happens best when managers and Masters are free to operate in a combination. We have discussed Masters, by seeing what they do and who they are; we have not discussed managers.

Managers are people who manage. They take care of the business at hand and they become involved in strategic planning. To do this, they must understand manufacturing development.

It is possible for such managers to come in from the outside, but rare. It is possible to have good managers who have not worked at manufacturing development, but rarer. In the long run it is not possible to have good managers who are not respected by the people, the Masters, who work with (not for) them.

Many managers come from a plant background, or from research, or from a business-oriented part of the company, but the good ones will have experienced all of these lives. This suggests that any Master of manufacturing development who wants to become a manager must leave his or her development role and wander purposefully into these other jobs/roles in order to prepare him- or herself. In the end, this suggests that the best manager will have all these experiences and also have been a Master of manufacturing development.

Let me assume that such are the managers we are going to talk about. They will have the respect of their peers (the Masters); know about the roots of technology from their time in development or earlier in research or at the least from their education; know about the plants and real life production problems and opportunities; and understand the power and constraints of money.

What about the managers of these managers? These people have to be responsible to the organization/company/ corporation that pays for the manufacturing development work. Let us assume a single individual for example, and one who has the respect of the managers and the Masters with whom he or she works. This person will need their support in establishing visions of the future, the person's main job.

No matter how the organization chart recognized by the company is structured, this person will be at their best if he or she works in the mental atmosphere of a truly horizontally structured system. When work is going on, all Masters are equal, including managers and any leader. When administration occupies the time available, the managers, and even more, the leader, are responsible for keeping the administrative load on working Masters to as low a level as possible.

I won't go on from here to argue the viability of such a dogmatic view or to discuss the management practices that have to ensue, but I will state that it is as possible as the human-nature limits of the Masters themselves will allow.

Consider how difficult it is (while in a hierarchically structured company where you are earning a salary) to contradict a person several (many) levels higher in authority even if you are his experience-equal in development. You have to be sure of yourself and of that person.

No one person is ever solely responsible for having vision, but a leader of managers generally has enough authority to establish a visionary effort, for two reasons. First, as stated, that person has the support of the people he or she works with, and second, has been appointed by a management which he or she works for and reports to, and therefore will be expected to judge and manage just how far into the future the Masters can stretch, and just what will be the paybacks for the company.

I have worked with people who are or were involved with visionary change. On the collective average of my experience, and in talking with people from large enough groups, there seems to be a visionary change started each year or so. By five years into each change process, either it was clear that the original vision was not thought out well enough and the work would fail, or redefinitions and hard work clarified new paths to success which generally included new visions.

Visionary change is usually cross-disciplinary, involving change in several technologies. It is possible to stretch for visionary change; to fail to reach far enough to succeed; and yet to succeed in creating advances in support technologies. Indeed it is not clear to me that visionary changes ever succeed if you are very strict in your examination, because you also have to ask if a vision which has to be redefined to make sense is a success or not. The only true answer comes years later, on the plant floor or in the company itself. Is there change?

There are many exciting new technologies around. If you can see the effect they will have in the future you are really pursuing a vision. If you cannot yet foresee an effect (on the plant floor; in the way we do things; for the company), you could still work on the technology but you would be doing research not development.

I have personally never seen a new technology, *chosen solely by a management team,* lead to a success, except when a particular individual or small team abstracted a clear new idea from the technology (the connecting rod example) On the other hand, I have seen several more complex technologies succeed in instances where there was *a vision shared by the individual Masters and the management team.* In other words, management cannot act alone.

Well then, here is an example written by Francis King who headed an organization called the MACE group (to be described) until very late 1991. He had been preceded by Derek Gentle who at the very beginning was preceded by Steve Weiner. The team started out without a name other than the "how to build a car" group and was very large at the outset. As it became clear what had to be done, the required team was easier to define and there was a reduction in size. This is another curious characteristic of good development: start large and narrow down. Don't start small and build. Now, Francis King's words.

Formation

In the world of automotive production, one of the most fundamental questions is "how to build a car". Simple as it sounds, this question, by all rights, should be the cornerstone of any manufacturing development in the automotive industry.

However, since we know how to build cars (of quality and at low cost), this question is not often seriously considered and was not pursued by us until we had established our own vision and purpose for manufacturing development. In retrospect, it is really a surprise that such a vision was not formed sooner, but only came some 35 years after the establishment of a research and development group at Ford.

A directive established externally by some upper management is ineffective in defining the mission or the goals of a manufacturing development program. That is especially true when the directive is in the form of a vision and is not driven by a need within the company, by a current problem on the plant floor, or by a technological idea.

To successfully define the mission of a program around the phrase "how to build a car", first, one needs to establish a team of diverse talents, because we all know the complexity of the vehicle product and the assorted means of producing a vehicle. Aside from the diversity of talents of the team, it also has to be sufficiently large to provide a critical mass of impact on the subject matter. Secondly, an environment has to be created for the team to function effectively. The environment has to stimulate new ideas, to be protective against intrusions or interruptions from requirements for help with current company problems, to encourage risk taking, to interact with other company experts in various fields, and to establish a link between manufacturing and product design/engineering.

Thirdly, and most importantly, the mission of the program must come from inside the team and not from an external source. The success of a team depends heavily on the personality of the team and the belief of the team in itself, its purpose, and in its development approach. Technical creativity complemented by dogged persistence is an important trait of the team. There is never sufficient resource or appreciation of the team's effort. Therefore, the team must possess the ability to utilize resources within and outside the company through excellent salesmanship.

Cultivation

The group, given a free charter and originally called Vehicle Assembly Operation Engineering, spent the first couple of years in understanding the assembly process and identifying problem areas of manufacturing. Complexity reduction, quality improvement, cost reduction, process consolidation, improved part commonality, and definitions for assembly were some of the identified areas of development in the early years. Partially because of the above established environment and team approach, these vast areas of development, as identified by the team, quickly led to a spectrum so broad that it encompassed the areas of component manufacturing, stamping, body construction, paint process, and trim/chassis assembly. This also included manufacturing-process-driven product designs chosen so that the manufacturing process could be implemented.

At such an early stage of program formation, creativity was encouraged by sheltering the development process from customer demands. Therefore, there was usually no customer buy-in for the projects and it was recognized that after the ideas had been developed, a concerted effort would be put forth to sell them.

As the group evolved during these formative years, it assumed a name more suitable to its charter, Manufacturing and Assembly Concepts Engineering (MACE). The charter became to develop, in a simultaneous engineering manner from a total systems point of view, manufacturing and assembly process concepts and process-driven product design concepts to enable the implementation of the processes. Even more simply put, the charter of the group became to envision, enable, and empower new manufacturing and assembly concepts.

Technological innovations

Through these years of cultivation, numerous technological innovations were investigated and spun-off to sub-teams or other individual developers outside MACE. [A list has been deleted here. It contained seven new single ideas most of which are being pursued/developed today.]

Concentration

As in all cases of development, there is a natural evolutionary path of expansion and convergence. Inherent in the breadth of the above referred to [deleted] list of technological innovations is the search for a focus or vision of the original meaning of the charter "how to build a car". By undertaking these numerous avenues of development, it became clear that even though there was no customer, let alone customer buy-in, for the development work, quantifiers were essential. The charter of "how to build a car" must be quantified by purposes like: for a lower cost, at higher customer satisfaction levels, in a shorter time, etc. A convergence back onto the charter of "how to build a car" with a specific purpose allowed the team to define a crisp vision and a focused sense of purpose. This new purpose addressed a possible need which may be realized in the future. The MACE team concentrated on defining an assembly process to build cars at low manufacturing costs for low-volume production, addressing the future need of market fragmentation.

With the realization of a purpose, the team pushed forward, with the help of a different kind of customer, Design Staff, in looking at alternative body construction techniques which would provide styling and model flexibility at low manufacturing costs. Surprisingly, and fortunately, the forming of this new vision did not force the team to start all over again. The foundation of much of the work had already been laid in the formation and cultivation periods. But now, with a renewed focus, the work was accomplished more rapidly.

Issues

Two crucial issues hindered the development process. When the MACE team was formed, the vision had been too narrow, partly because the team consisted only of manufacturing engineers, albeit with design experience. To investigate alternative body construction techniques, new body construction designs were required. Inadequacy of talent in the product development arena was a serious problem. Some of the key product design and analysis work had to be outsourced beyond the control of the team. As a consequence, inadequate funding surfaced as the second issue, either for money to build the team or to pay for better outsourced work.

Cooperation with suppliers

A key solution was arranged without much extra money. Outside suppliers were requested to become part of the team to assist with project development. In all of the aforementioned projects [deleted], different suppliers were part of the team, assisting not only technically but also in some instances financially through provision of experimental tooling and/or material. In the alternative body construction program, not only was the team able to involve outside suppliers, it was also able to obtain direct assistance from its customer.

Corporate consciousness – the outcome

Customer willingness to be involved in a program comes from the sharing of a common belief, goal, and vision with the development team. Design Staff became convinced that in order for Ford to continue design leadership in the industry, alternative body construction methods would be required. Because of this belief, Design Staff, our customer, has significantly raised the level of consciousness about alternative body construction methods at all levels of corporate management.

The body construction method proposed by the team has been exhibited within Ford worldwide. A migration plan for the method has been formulated, but the ultimate success of a development program is implementation – in this case, of an alternative body construction concept – and it is still too early to determine success. Nevertheless, from the advanced manufacturing development team's point of view, it succeeded in broadcasting to the rest of the company that alternatives exist in "how to build a car".

Comments

This overview of the MACE activity describes something quite different from the plant problem – no customer; no plant; no plant people; no clear changes at the start. It seems that a search is a fundamental part of the process in "the vision of new technology". When a general question such as "how to build a car" is asked, the combination of managers and Masters mentioned earlier works best. All together these people can ask collectively: What can we do today that is different? What would we need to develop in order to facilitate a different way of doing things (i.e. what new technologies are needed)? Has someone else in another field done this? Are there tools available? Do we have the resources? (the managers especially must ask this and the next two questions) Is it in the company's interest? Can we see a path to eventual customers?

A summary of all this in fact describes the role of managers in manufacturing development. Much of their work is pure administration which has rules and will obey norms. In this area they do best when they facilitate the work of Masters; they help when asked, and do not hinder. Some of their work approaches being an art when new technologies and visions for the future are in question. Then there can be powerful results from a team of people if it is a *team of managers and Masters, working as equals and searching for a new way.*

♦   ♦

In summary, there is a prescription for management which also adds to a description of what manufacturing development is:

- The rules for success (i.e. the first and second prescriptions) must be recognized, acknowledged and pursued.
- For any manufacturing development success, managers must have the respect of the Masters.
- "The mental atmosphere" of a truly horizontally structured system must operate in the workplace regardless of the formal organization structure.
- Plant problems and new ideas once identified must be pursued by Masters and administratively helped by managers.
- New technologies should only be chosen and pursued when there is a *vision* truly shared by individual Masters and the management team.
- The *vision of a new technology* must be appropriate to the company or corporation, or the development work may be in jeopardy because it cannot become real.
- The pursuit of an even larger *vision* which may involve several new technologies requires a search by com-

binations of people who have managerial as well as technical responsibilities.

- Only in an exceptional instance is a customer desirable at the *vision* stage.
- Teamwork is essential.

SOME PRECAUTIONS AGAINST FAILURE

Are there any worthy failures?

I believe there are no worthy failures in development work. If you fail, you fail. That's it.

Visions fail when managers and Masters do not work together. New technologies fail if you don't extract a single new idea. New ideas fail if you don't find a customer. Masters who attempt to solve plant problems never fail. They are Masters because they succeed.

Masters must focus on success; it is in the nature of their art. But, managers have a different role and must be conscious of failure as a possibility.

I will, therefore, introduce one *new technology* example with a specific purpose here. It failed and then it succeeded. There is a lesson in it. It seems there can be an antidote for failure. The description was written by its longest-serving team member Hossein Nivi, who helped to find the antidote.

Background

During 1981 a group at the Manufacturing Development Center (MDC) proposed development of a new transmission test stand to the Transmission and Chassis (T&C) Division for their new overdrive transaxle transmission created for the all new car line later called Taurus and Sable. This proposal recommended a new approach (i.e. a new technology) to transmission test stand technology by replacing a flywheel on the output shaft (which *partially* represented vehicle inertia) and an absorber at the output of the transmission with a controllable motor (see Figure 5). These actions allowed energy to be pumped from both ends of the transmission in selected portions of the test cycle to reduce the cycle time.

An exact understanding of test stand principles is not necessary to understand the change. What you are trying to achieve is a machine or fixture that acts on a transmission (or reacts to a transmission) close to the action of a car it will serve. That is, the transmission being tested thinks it is in a real car on a real road. We had come closer.

The project

The proposal projected 35–40 percent reduction in cycle time which translates to 35–40 percent reduction in number of test stands. Another existing line we used for comparison needed 20 test stands to keep up with production, at a cost of approximately $800,000 each. So the cost savings were substantial if the new technology was feasible. T&C management decided to establish feasibility evaluation. It was decided to give a production type

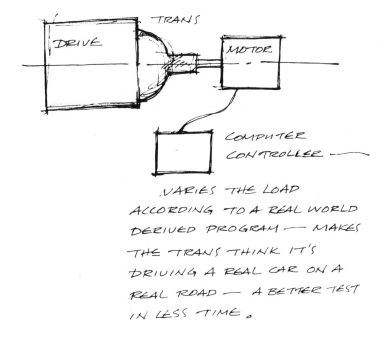

TRANS

DRIVE

MOTOR

COMPUTER
CONTROLLER ———

.VARIES THE LOAD
ACCORDING TO A REAL WORLD
DERIVED PROGRAM — MAKES
THE TRANS THINK IT'S
DRIVING A REAL CAR ON A
REAL ROAD — A BETTER TEST
IN LESS TIME.

Figure 5   Transmission testing with a real world derived program

test stand, which was not in use, to MDC and let them prove the concept. (Notice it was a management decision . . . and that the prove-out was to be at MDC, not at the plant.)

Over the same period, Ford was going through a dramatic transformation, with upper management strongly advocating team participation and employee involvement. Therefore a team of people from the Livonia Plant and T&C Division was formed to determine specifications, select vendors and determine the technology to be used.

MDC members were invited to participate in this team and shape the future of the test technology. But most of us hadn't worked in such broad teams before, so it seemed that the technologists (MDC), the plant people, and the Division staff each had their own agendas to follow. Specifically, the relation between MDC and the rest of the team was adversarial. The MDC staff were looked on as people with extra university degrees; they didn't have real plant deadlines; etc. As technologists, it appeared (and it was at least partly true) that we wanted to set up the specifications and features to accommodate our specific technology and did not pay enough attention to the concerns of plant people who had to maintain the test systems on the plant floor.

On the other hand, the plant and division people (it appeared to the MDC people) were happy to continue with the conventional technology that they were comfortable with, and that their favorite vendor would support.

The final element of this relationship was that it seemed the supplier would lose substantial business if the new technology was implemented.

A two-prong approach was then adopted. (This was a root cause for failure because this resulted in two teams.) MDC would develop and demonstrate the new concept with reduced cycle time; and T&C would develop the specification based on the conventional technology. By the end of 1982 a decision would be made on which approach should be adopted. (This is almost a set of conditions for a contest between teams; not a contest for technologies within one team.)

MDC was under pressure to develop and demonstrate the new technology in less than one year. Remember that this was a non-deadline accustomed group. A very talented team of engineers, software developers, mechanical designers, and technicians was nevertheless formed to make a concentrated effort and deliver the new technology. Midway through the development, Sam Schmuter, one of the lead engineers, made a simple and conceptual proposal: "since we have added motors to the output shaft and control these motors by a computer, we should be able to do more than come close to the action of the car, we should be able to simulate the vehicle inertia any way we want." This idea not only compensated for eliminating the flywheel and partial vehicle inertia mentioned earlier, it simulated full-vehicle inertia and realistic road conditioning on the test stand.

This ideas was so intriguing that a good deal of engineering effort was devoted to see if it was workable. So, even though it was very good, a new idea had "intruded" during a deadlined development. Solving a problem and fulfilling a need of the division had become instead a *vision* of simulating a vehicle and a realistic road.

This type of idea had always been desirable but a mechanical, full-vehicle, inertia had always (until the active computer) meant a substantial increase in the cycle time. N. Field, V. Milenkovic, H. Nivi and S. Schmuter worked on this concept and perfected it. They also patented it for Ford, showing that conflicting constraints, "reducing cycle time" and "testing with full vehicle inertia", were now living side by side. A modular software concept for the test cycle was also adopted to make future changes easy and manageable.

The failure

The original concept plus the full-vehicle inertia simulation was fully demonstrated on the modified production test stand (that T&C management had given to MDC) before the end of 1982. This meant a team of about 10 people working for very long hours, seven days a week for many months. The results were a great success as far as technical issues were concerned. They were, however, unproved as far as the plant was concerned, because many issues such as durability and maintainability remained unanswered.

Division staff and plant people had worked with their vendor and had decided on "what needs to be done". The final recommendation of the overall team did not entirely ignore MDC's work. That recommendation was to continue with conventional technology and to borrow a few of the concepts involved in the new technology, such as putting motors on the output shaft and later some of the software concepts.

Details have not been included, but on both sides all this was a very good example of how not to form a team. Even when the concept of the team is enforced, team members have to learn how to work together. Enforcing a concept is not the right way; people have to adopt the concept not adapt to it. This was probably also a classic case of conflicts of ego and interests.

♦ ♦

An antidote

During 1983, 1984, and 1985, a much reduced MDC team continued additional development on transmission testing, also at a much reduced resource level. They became convinced that issues of maintainability and durability could be resolved and tried to find ways so that T&C Division would adopt this technology.

Once you fail, the barriers are higher than ever. So the technology had to be expanded to make it more inviting than ever. The concept of a flexible test stand which can test a variety of front- and rear-wheel drive transmissions on the same hardware was developed. A substantial number of diagnostic tests for early detection of many production problems were developed.

The antidote to failure is to form a new team without any of the original members, or at least without recognizable ones. During 1987 a customer was found. This was an engineer (manager) in T&C staff named Dave Wood, who formed a new team with many new faces from T&C to take advantage of this new technology. This time MDC chose the stance of being a consultant to the team and, rather than telling the T&C team what to do, MDC responded to their needs and T&C could see themselves as the owner and champion of the new test technology.

Jim Dana of T&C finally led the team to obtain management approval for a pilot facility to put all the concepts of flexible hardware, software, and diagnostic together. At the heart of the new test system was the inertia simulation concept.

The pilot test facility was successfully launched at the Livonia Product Development test facility during 1990. The Batavia plant in 1992 was the first one to receive new test stands based on inertia simulation and all the other concepts built up during the decade; the Van Dyke plant subsequently implemented this technology in 1993.

Comments

Let us review what you need for the application of a new idea and couple that with the "test stand technology" in 1982:

- to find a customer **wrong one**
- plant people to genuinely want new technology **no success**
- to be known to the plant people **wrong way**
- to be expert **yes**
- enough change to make a difference **yes**
- a pilot involving plant people **no**
- to give credit to the plant **no**

- to exit gracefully   **no**
- to be "lucky"   **no**

This comparison speaks for itself. It took eight more years (which was perhaps three more than starting from scratch) to repair the flaws in the approach of the development team. But it wasn't the individuals, nor was it the team itself. It seems to me that the flaw was in the management part of the process. The managers and Masters didn't work together, in that: the managers failed to advise the development team that there was no plant problem and that a challenge or need had to be developed; and the plant didn't really want new technology. And then the managers didn't do something about the circumstances when the development work left the one-idea stage and blossomed into a *vision*. In fact, it seems that the Masters were not Masters in 1982, and the managers did not manage. I can't draw any other conclusion.

The antidote here was to persevere after reviewing the conditions which led to failure in the first try. There is no antidote that has anything to do with the way your customers (in the plant) act; it has to do with a clarification of what you do and who you are.

The precautions are . . . Do not confuse a "vision of new technology" with manufacturing development . . . Do not compete with customers . . . Let Masters be Masters and teach managers how to manage people who work at an art.

The precautions are: learn the three prescriptions and use them. Here they are repeated in one place for emphasis.

Prescription One: for Success in Manufacturing Development

A team or an individual needs:

- to reduce new technologies to the level of one new idea
- to find a customer
- the plant people to positively want new technology (easiest if there is a plant problem)
- to be known to the plant people
- to be expert
- enough change to make a difference
- a pilot involving plant people
- to give credit to the plant
- to exit gracefully, and
- to be "lucky" – to be a Master (see Two).

Prescription Two: for becoming a Master

Individuals need to:

- have belief and remain students
- learn by doing
- choose tasks that suit them
- choose the right targets
- concentrate on success
- let successes speak for themselves, and
- have the inner strength to spend years.

Prescription Three: for Success in the Management of Development

Managements must be aware that:

- the rules for success (i.e. the first and second prescriptions) must be recognized, acknowledged and pursued
- for any manufacturing development success, managers must have the respect of the Masters
- "the mental atmosphere" of a truly horizontally structured system must operate in the workplace regardless of the formal organization structure
- plant problems and new ideas once identified must be pursued by Masters and administratively helped by managers. New technologies should only be chosen and pursued when there is a Vision truly shared by individual Masters and the management team
- the Vision of a new technology must be appropriate to the company or corporation, or the development work may be in jeopardy because it cannot become real
- the pursuit of an even larger Vision which may involve several new technologies requires a search by combinations of people who have managerial as well as technical responsibilities
- only in an exceptional instance is a customer desirable at the Vision stage
- teamwork is essential

What do winners have that losers don't?

The first two prescriptions are written for individuals especially the second one which is essentially the description of a Master. They could, however, equally apply to teams if everyone on a team recognizes each element, and the beginners or journeymen who work on teams recognize the Masters whom they should observe and learn from.

A Master is almost always required. This Master knows the times when he or she cannot do the job alone and so, without question from managers but, on the contrary, with their help, he or she forms a team. The team will be successful if the team acts as an individual.

Winners have teams that act as one

Sure they have arguments. Sure it takes time. Sure teams can break up (afterwards), but when they are winners they act as one. Not all members of a team are Masters of manufacturing development. Some are administrators, facilitators, assistants, secretaries; but when they are winners they are treated and treat each other as equals and they act as one.

I know of no other single factor that can be identified as interconnecting the characteristics of successful manufacturing development teams – those from the staffs, the plants, management, and so on – they act as one.

A precaution against failure is to examine the attitude within teams. Do not attempt to control a team from the outside – it will not then "act as one". At the best this advice is a precaution and, hopefully, not an antidote. This advice applies to almost everyone and for management is possibly even an addendum to the third prescription.

What is a pilot and what isn't a pilot?

The first prescription calls for "a pilot involving plant people". I have seen some projects fail at the pilot stage because of inept management, some because the practitioners involved were not yet Masters (remember a Master is almost always required), and some because no one involved seemed to know what a pilot or pilot program was. Let me assume all the other parts of the first prescription are in hand and attempt to explain a pilot program.

A pilot program for an idea, a technology, a machine, etc., or more simply a pilot, is a transition in manufacturing development. The Masters of manufacturing development who narrow down a new technology to apply one new idea (with the help of managers) and who then focus on a plant application will already have involved plant people at the floor, staff, and management level. The proportion or the character of the plant people (i.e. just who: hourly; engineers; supervisors; all of these) will depend largely on the personal style of the Master. Of course, if the team is working on an invention needed to solve a plant problem that proportion will already be largely a given; remember the plant is "dying" and who will "die" worst will be most involved and most interested.

Up until the pilot it will have been manufacturing development. At the pilot stage it starts to become manufacturing.

You are going into the plant. Or, the plant is coming to your floor to replicate itself.

You have been learning from success. Now you are prepared to "learn from failure". You are going to try something that you are convinced will be successful, but the unknown of the plant and the nature of its machinery have to be faced. The plant people learn from mistakes in order to learn how to avoid them, to regularize, to find and avoid the conditions that lead to breakdowns, long repair time, and a myriad other undesirables.

The Master of manufacturing development has to carry through his (or her; and afterwards he or she) work to implementation on the plant floor or he is not a Master. He is a member (now) of the plant team. He is a relay runner on a second-last lap and must smoothly hand over the baton, making sure all the while that neither he nor his partner lose a step. He must run part of the last lap with his (new) partner to ensure a successful transition. He must run at his partner's pace. He must softly (gracefully) loosen his grip and go to the inside of the track to applaud his teammate onward.

There might be misleading points in this metaphor (even though I have found it very appealing and understandable in public talks), so I will go back to the real world, where manufacturing development is in transition and becoming manufacturing:

- A pilot has to involve people.
- A pilot is a preliminary (or experimental) trial, because the real trial occurs when a process is first run in production.
- A pilot must nevertheless involve the people who will eventually run the process (idea, part of a new technology, computer, machine, etc.) in production.
- A pilot must somehow involve everyone; exclusions will cause problems in the future.
- A pilot has to involve people who have transferred or will transfer. When a pilot is run in the production plant the development people must live there (not just be visitors). When a pilot is run elsewhere (e.g. at a development center), the production people as well as the engineers from the plant must be there and run the pilot.
- A pilot (in a plant) can be run off-line (i.e. parallel to, but not interfering with current production) but the results must be fed into production. Here there will be massive rules about testing and identifying/following

parts/items that went through the pilot segment; this is administration.

- A pilot has to use equipment as close as possible to that which will go into production.
- A pilot is run by a team that must include suppliers, machine builders, customers for the part/process as well as the overall final development team (plant and masters).
- A pilot should be run by a team that enjoys its work. It should in fact have fun and this is a challenge for both Masters *and* managers.

A preliminary trial that does not meet the foregoing conditions is not a pilot. But this is not all; the best pilots are run as a Zen monastery was organized: "To every member, except the abbot, was assigned some special work in the caretaking of the monastery, and curiously enough, to the novices were committed the lighter duties, while to the most respected and advanced monks were given the more irksome and menial tasks." (*The Book of Tea*, Kakuzo Okakura, 1906) In other words the Masters of manufacturing development must be there; must work at their own ideas; and must not hand over until they have done the toughest and worst critical work. They must also help the team succeed by respecting the essence of a spirit of politeness which requires that you say what you are expected to say, and no more.

All the preceding points apply to plants, the people in them and the interaction of manufacturing development people.

However, there are occasions with *new* *technologies* that border on *visions* where a different kind of pilot is necessary to show that several identifiable single new ideas can be extracted. The words of Pete Sferro describe this in dealing with stereolithography.

Where did it begin?

Ford's Design Center had a program called 2000X which was to identify new ways to improve the present methods used to create models of new vehicles. Mr Giuliano Zuccato from the 2000X project was in California looking at the movie industry for triggers on new technologies to make model cars when he came across a newly issued patent on stereolithography. At that time (Autumn 1986) the process could only make a solid object (2 in.) from math equations. Giuliano thought that this method could be developed to make model cars or at least parts of them in much less time than the present methods used in design studios.

The process of stereolithography utilizes a laser light to cure liquid photo polymers in very thin layers. Each layer corresponds to a cross-sectional slice in a computer file from a computer-aided design (CAD) model. This technology reduces very complex three dimensional geometric models to a simple two dimensional environment by slicing the model into very thin slices (0.005–0.020 in.), then creates the surface area of each slice while matching the thickness of the slice by the speed of the laser across the liquid photo polymer. This replicates the slice by drawing two dimensionally across the surface of the liquid. Each slide is bonded together by the material itself, creating a replica of the CAD math model out of plastic (see Figure 6).

Early customer buy-in

Initially Giuliano could not find anyone to support the idea that this technology would ever be capable of making models rapidly

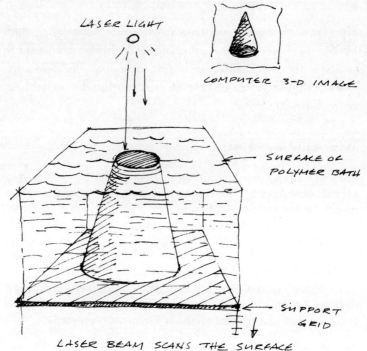

LASER LIGHT

COMPUTER 3-D IMAGE

SURFACE OF POLYMER BATH

SUPPORT GRID

LASER BEAM SCANS THE SURFACE
OF THE POLYMER BATH, GUIDED BY THE
COMPUTER GENERATED IMAGE OF THE FORM,
POLYMERIZING A THIN LAYER OF THE RESIN
IN THE SHAPE OF A SECTION OR "SLICE" OF
THE FORM THE SUPPORT GRID STEPS DOWN,
SUBMERGING THE NEWLY SOLIDIFIED SURFACE —
ANOTHER SLICE IS FORMED BY A SECOND
PASS OF THE LASER BEAM — AND SO ON —
FORMING A SOLID, ONE "SLICE" AT A TIME.

Figure 6   The process of stereolithography

from CAD. Research people did not think that the polymer technology was there to support the requirements of making good parts and management didn't believe that it could be done. It seemed that everyone focused on what couldn't be done.

By February of 1987 he had talked to many people and had finally arranged for a technology evaluation trip to California by a cross-functional team of engineers. Chuck Feltner of MDC (one of the managers) called me late on a Sunday night asking me to go to California the next day to see if there was any potential in this new technology called "stereolithography". I joined the team to review the technology and we agreed that there was a lot of potential in the new method.

The team members reported to their respective managements that they felt that this technology had potential in the future and recommended that Ford get involved in the development of it. Then nothing happened for four months, which I found quite frustrating. So I started personally to take on the task of developing a project to bring this technology into Ford, contacting the engineers interested in the technology to get their ideas and their buy-in support to become part of the development project.

Once this was accomplished, I approached my management with a proposal to start a project. MDC people were used to focusing on what *could* be done, not on what couldn't. Money was the only problem. So this management gave permission to proceed with the project, with the condition that all initial project funding and support engineers should come from the operating divisions in a new type of pilot – a *new technology pilot*. We set up a series of presentations to the chief engineers of ten divisions with the help of grass roots engineers from each division, asking management for:

- a high level manager to be part of a steering committee to act as the corporate guidance of this technology;
- an engineer to work on the development of it; and
- a cost sharing of the build and launch at MDC.

Initially seven activities participated in the project to launch the pilot. Most of the managements indicated that they did not expect the project to be a success but because the team really believed in it, they went along with it.

Everyone on the team (we narrowed down initially to five engineers) did believe in the technology and would do whatever it took to make it work. The program was set up so that MDC would work on the technology issues, and engineers from the operations would work on the applications methodologies. Everyone would receive the same training and would be capable of doing any job on the project. All project work would be applied to present engineering car programs to show cost benefits early in the project development in order to gain continuing support. This technology would be transferred into the divisions through their respective engineers' participation in the program. These were the guidelines set up by the team itself.

The program's first success came just one month after the equipment was installed. One division built one small part (i.e. one demonstrable *new idea*) which saved them three months development time and $30,000. Their first-year contribution to the program was $25,000 which they saved on their first part. The program took off like a rocket from there, with another division saving $3 million on just one design which went into production.

Personalities

The team had many different types of people, but we complemented each other. All were very persistent, some even working on the project when their management had told them not to; all were willing to do more than their share and to merge their special talents; it was an all-the-way task – to do whatever it took to get the job done. This project team found ways to overcome all obstacles that got in the way of its success. Sometimes they cut corners, pushed the "system" to its limits, but they never crossed the lines of ethics, friendship, and good sense.

Implementation

This program was started with transfer and implementation as the main objective. Hence, each participating activity had their own engineers trained in all aspects of the program from "day one". These engineers are now the champions in their respective operations on the implementation of this technology in the company. One division has now launched their own laboratory; another is in the process of purchasing their equipment; five other activities are in the process of developing their own projects; facilities in England and Germany are to be launched, and Ford of Australia is working with the MDC team to prove feasibility in FOA. (This was late 1991; the technology is now widespread, more complex, more used, and more exciting.)

Comments

This program has been the basis for several others in the manufacturing development arena at Ford and has been one trigger for the Rapid Response Manufacturing Consortium described in the Appendix (as a second example of a *vision*). What do we learn?

Programs and even pilots, which by nature are transitional, must be run by people who focus on success, who always look at what can be done, and who don't waste time criticizing what can't be done. Concentrate on success. Following the mood established right from the beginning of this book, it can be stated emphatically that: **Masters of manufacturing development concentrate on success.**

ARE THERE ANY OTHER RULES?

For individuals

The title of this concluding section is set as another question because I believe there must be other rules. Three prescriptions have been set out for success and a few precautions were specially noted to make sure that particular steps in these prescriptions don't get missed. For example, even though it is very uncommon, you don't absolutely need a manufacturing development team, but the Master has to form a team with the plant. This observation is based on real experience but it is hard to form a rule from it. Therefore, I am going to add a few more observations and comments that might guide others and might even have rules hidden somewhere.

First, we need some reminders, some generalities. Remember that manufacturing is immense (some comparisons will be given in the next chapter) and that manufacturing development is a tiny part of this. Remember that few people even know about manufacturing development or what it is.

There has been no discussion of trouble-shooting and almost no discussion about applications work, which are both part of manufacturing life. In trouble-shooting it is clear that the plant has a problem and wants help. In applications work it is general that someone (someone else) has created a method or a process or developed an idea. In applying an idea that has worked elsewhere you will work in less jeopardy of failure. You are not trying to prove an idea at the same time as applying it to production. So in one case, trouble-shooting, you have the problem and no solution; in the case of applications, a solution and perhaps no problem.

Trouble-shooting implies trouble. No good manager will send a beginner out to trouble-shoot. A beginner can go along to learn with a Master, the seasoned hand who knows the plant floor and has a wealth of technologies and personal contacts. A beginner cannot trouble-shoot alone. If the trouble-shooting fails, the beginner will be marked by the group he was sent to; he or she will be discouraged; and the manager who let it happen will be known as a non-contributor.

On the other hand, to watch a Master of manufacturing development size up a problem is an ideal situation for learning. A beginner can see the plant, the Master and observe the attitudes of people.

For a beginner to work on applications is alright but can be seductively diverting. If you assume that the beginner has all the required credentials showing the basis (knowledge) to allow him or her eventually to become a Master and you encourage him or her to work on applications, he or she will be copying or expanding the work of someone (at a remove) who may be a Master but who is not around to be a role model. The value of a Master to a beginner is as a purveyor of style, a teacher of method, a storehouse of experience . . . not as someone who had an idea (the person whose idea you are to apply) and who has left the scene.

It is valuable to keep on with these outside topics of trouble-shooting and applications. One of the challenges in dealing with a new technology is the same as a problem for the individual in dealing with an application. If there is no problem, there is no solution. With a new idea you have the drive to express yourself by applying something you yourself have done. When you apply someone else's idea or work an idea out of someone else's new technology (remember: decided on by Masters and managers) there can be a lessened driving force. This is common but not necessary.

There are very good people/engineers who work on applications whom I have excluded here when I excluded applications work. Applications work is most often pursued by people who would be impatient with Zen-like ideas. They are "action people"; they don't want to "spend years on a project". I don't blame them; successful applications are enjoyable and rewarding.

I do not exclude trouble-shooting. This type of challenge keeps all engineers, whether or not they are applications people or Masters of manufacturing development, alive.

Trouble-shooting, or the encounter with a real plant problem that the plant people cannot solve themselves, is by definition an encounter with the unknown. It is thus a trigger to invention at least equal to any other trigger I know.

A beginner sent out to trouble-shoot with a Master is new to manufacturing development but can be many different people. For example, there is the new hire direct from school; there is the plant person rotated into a development area for training; there is a professor who leaves university on a sabbatical to experience another world. However, I believe that only one of these examples will become a Master of manufacturing development. Rotations imply shorter times and one of the keys for a master developer is to have the inner strength to spend years. The plant person who returns and the professor who goes back after the sabbatical are on rotation. They are not committed.

Perhaps there is another question to be asked. Is there a profession of manufacturing development? It has been said that it is unwise to let a job become a profession because someone else defines a job, and a profession by definition must be self-defined.

Well then, are there any observations for people who are not working as Masters, but who are in close contact with these professionals? It seems there are two.

For the beginner

Be attached to a Master in order to learn.

For managers and leaders

Be aware of what a Master is. Here is an opportunity to repeat part of the first prescription, after using ideas from the third one. First, assume that the "manager" to be discussed is personable, knows administrative rules, is versed in employee involvement and actually likes people (very important to me, personally, but I have seen winners who didn't). This manager has to understand who a Master of manufacturing development is (i.e. "the way to success"), what he knows (i.e. his expertise), and be clear about the conditions under which success will come easiest.

Then he or she must ensure that the Master matches the problem, that the Master is an expert known to the plant people and that he or she knows how to define his or her customers and ensure that the plant people really want new technology. Here *ensure* means *help make sure*. Then the manager must judge or arrange that there is:

- enough change to make a difference (not trouble-shooting) . . . an invention;
- a pilot involving plant people where the right (accepted) methods are used;
- as much credit given to the plant as possible; and
- a graceful exit without applause – others will applaud if there is success.

The manager will already have ensured "luck" by choosing the right Master.

There are at least a hundred points that could be made about managers. In effect, we just said that the manager's first job in manufacturing development was to know his area of company responsibilities and to match the set of company needs that he sees to the people who work *with* him, and especially to recognize Masters and assign all others to work with them. The other ninety-nine tasks are parts of management and not necessarily of manufacturing development.

What about leaders? For success in a company, or any other organization that can fund manufacturing development, the leader must be adept at blending outside pressures with inside roles. The leader must understand the plant floor and his management, which are both outside the manufacturing development function. The leader must be conscious of the role to be played in the sense that "consciousness is needed in order to form new judgments . . . where the rules have not been laid down beforehand". The leader must on the other hand be capable of supporting his colleagues in an automatic way (where consciousness is not needed), so that they can pursue success without being worried about what the administration will think.

Depending on the company, the managers, the times (i.e. is the industry mature or changing), and the emphasis placed on manufacturing development, different types of leaders will be required. Manufacturing support in terms of applications is not manufacturing development, but good manufacturing support is certainly preferable to bad manufacturing development, and the leader must be responsible for choosing the road to be traveled. The rules are unclear; they are probably more management rules than guiding rules for manufacturing development.

♦ ♦

I write about the search for other rules very personally. I had the opportunity to be a leader and have now chosen to go on to a university. Twenty years ago in the United States there were almost no schools that taught courses in manufacturing. One of the first several-day meetings on the topic held at the Carnegie Mellon University and sponsored by the National Science Foundation had to be described by a title that did not use the word manufacturing in order to be sponsored. Today, there are dozens of universities granting degrees with the word "manufacturing" in them. It is not clear to me whether manufacturing is indeed a profession or is instead a discipline to be practiced by people who are professionals fundamentally taught in other schools of endeavor. I intend to find out. Perhaps then I will be able to recommend who the leaders of manufacturing development might be. They are not as clearly recognizable as the Masters. Perhaps we could say that the abbot must be laical if the Masters are to be allowed a secular life. How then do you train the abbot?

For the manufacturing enterprise

Manufacturing is hard to look at at any one instant. Not because it is elusive, but because it is immense. Some plants are so large you can truly get lost in them. Some use enough electricity to provide functions for a modern city of 200,000 people. The computer which is a complex tool gets lost among many other tools of comparable complexity on a plant floor.

In another cut at immensity, let us consider that there are at least ten basic divisions of manufacturing processes. If the cut is made so that "joining" is one of those divisions, you can then subdivide joining into at least ten categories. Welding will be one of these. You will then find that there are eighty-five separate welding processes recognized by the American Welding Society. This cascade gives us $10 \times 10 \times 85$ ($= 8,500$) and is mostly representative, so I can state that there are five to ten thousand separately recognizable manufacturing processes.

A thorough examination could illustrate the immensity of manufacturing in many other ways, but the best stress that can be laid is to note the difficulty of managing it. (This is noted instead of being explained because the explanation is itself immense. Please read the myriad of books published in the last decade about manufacturing to see if they can tell you "how to manage manufacturing".)

If one accepts manufacturing as immense, then development of new concepts (change) must be a smaller part. This will include applications of others' already successfully applied ideas, evolutionary changes, process improvements; stresses on concepts like quality, flexibility; new controls using the computer and procedures from statistics; and so on. Manufacturing development as used in this book is thus only a tiny part of a smaller part of manufacturing. My estimate for manufacturing development is that it exists as a fraction of one percent of manufacturing.

Perhaps the smallness of this fraction can help explain why a company can decide to pursue a process that requires at least equal parts of belief and bottom line.

There is nevertheless a minimum investment. There is a minimum size related to the need for Masters to have other Masters to talk to. (The Cornish language died before the last person who could speak Cornish died. There must be someone to talk to in order to have a real language.) The minimum relates to the bottom line. As will be noted, not every program attempted by a group of manufacturing developers proves to be a financial success. Statistically then, financial successes will be spread out in time as well as in topic area.

There is a difference between administrators and manufacturing development managers; the administrator may not have the patience of the manager (usually a once-Master). The stability of a manufacturing development enterprise, therefore, will require a large enough portfolio of work so that success can flow at a reasonably regular (and profitable) rate. This requires enough people.

My experience says that a successful enterprise needs at least 20 to 30 people even for a small range of manufacturing endeavors. At the other extreme you will become almost too large beyond 130 to 150 people. Example factors to consider are that everyone should know everyone else in order to get at an optimum for the best team operation; and thus there will be an upper limit.

One curiosity is that the managers must be able to protect against the demands of success. If you are successful in delivering a new idea, the implementation will require more people, and then there are fewer left to develop other new ideas.

Finally, as a thought drawn from Zen, there must be *sword makers*. In the last chapter of *Zen in the Art of Archery*, Herrigel talks about Japanese sword Masters who also approach their art as do Japanese archers . . . in the way of Zen. Among these Masters is a fundamental reliance and great respect for the men who make their weapons, the swords. In manufacturing development the Masters also need great support from weapon makers: from machinists, electricians, millwrights, foundry helpers and the many others needed for work in a plant (or plant-like) environment. So the minimum number of people also involves the range of support required.

◆   ◆

Let me now reflect on manufacturing development as a recognizable function in a manufacturing enterprise. Consider the meeting point for manufacturing development with administration on the overall level. This administration is upper management or involves responding and reporting to higher management. It deals with problems on the enterprise level. If detail must be examined, the administrator will focus on anti-failure not on success, and this has to be avoided. A leader of manufacturing development who must respond to and also represent the administration has to be a semi-permeable membrane, letting through some concerns but not others on the detail level. On the overall level the leader must examine profit, be concerned with concepts like zero-based budgets, must determine optimum sizes, and be an efficient administrator.

There is a last item which is especially interesting: this manufacturing development leader must know and measure the *value of protection*. With a large enough group of people (including the Masters) it is possible to look at new processes forced by opportunity or by regulation, or to look at the best timing for massive change, a difficult challenge (both of these are forms of the *vision* for *new technology*). One allowable result of this looking must always be a decision not to act.

If not acting is not an option for the results from manufacturing development, the development will be restrained and there will be a focus on failure, not on success. I will not describe the projects involved but want to mention that successes in the painting of automobiles, by Masters of manufacturing development at Ford, have involved both the adoption of massive changes in technology as well as decisions not to adopt, or in other words, decisions to avoid certain changes. These Masters worked very closely with plant people in the operations. What they did was to protect the company by examining some technologies quite thoroughly and then recommending against them. Their work and knowledge served *to protect the company from lack of choice.*

The team of people I worked with covered a large range of manufacturing development. There were enough people to produce hundreds of results a year. Many of these were results in trouble-shooting or the advising equivalent that we usually call consulting. Some outputs bordered on research. There was preliminary work done to investigate new ideas or technologies that didn't "make the headlines." These were eliminated, not just because the new idea wasn't a good one, but because manufacturing development (as defined here) must involve implementation on the plant floor and future implementation could not be envisioned. The Master of manufacturing development must have some of the necessary pragmatism that is in a manufacturing person – not only must the idea work, but it has to be a significant improvement and this involves the bottom line. So the cut between research and manufacturing development is made at the need for implementation and the requirement for a visibly profitable improvement.

From these hundreds of results, we decided together each year which were especially notable and from these a handful each year were designated as landmarks. So in eight years with this group, there were about fifty significant projects or landmarks which have been examined in detail. This examination was as critical as we could make it, but not one I would like to defend in court with a bunch of physicists sitting on the jury. The results are:

plant problems	100 percent successes
new ideas	
new technologies	60/90 percent successes
visions	30 percent successes

You can see that our *vision* was often cloudy but our response to a *plant problem* was right-on. The range for *new ideas* and *new technologies* depended on how well we were able to establish the one new idea to work on out of a new technology.

Our success rate was as high as it appears, not just because of what we chose to do, but also because of what we chose not to do and what we chose to stop early enough. (The focus on success by a manufacturing development Master involves an analysis of financial impact; and here we worked as a team of self-critics.)

The numbers have been given for one purpose, to compliment the Masters. When the Masters did what they were best at doing, success resulted. When a team of managers got into the act to help select new technologies or "had visions" the results were less certain. But change cannot always be small, an idea at a time – and there is a definite role for managers. Here I believe it lies in the choices of what not to do and of what to stop early enough.

A reflection on exceptional people and groups

Most of this book has been anecdotal and this last chapter will go to an extreme, as you will see. The book could have been otherwise, without Zen, as a set of organized case histories and tabulated results reasoned from observation. But "the tea room is made for the tea Master, not the tea Master for the tea room."

There are few heroes and few villains in most of our lives. Manufacturing development is no exception, yet to me the Masters are heroes. They devote much of themselves to doing what they do.

Sometimes someone who looks like a Master and produces success even though he is not a Master goes unrecognized. Years ago when I worked for another company doing research, there was a particular researcher whom I found first rate and who taught me a lot. He was what I have called "a blackboard". When you talked to him you wrote on him, and you could begin to see your problem or whatever the issue was, because it was brought out for examination, put forward to see.

His office was around the corner from a bigger lab. When you walked along the outside corridor you could partly see into his office. There were often people in his office, talking, drinking coffee, arguing. Although he did publish work this man was not prolific. He didn't have the time because we were always there, arguing and drinking coffee.

Management who were otherwise good people walked along the hallways like anyone else and they saw the coffee groups in his office. Being scientists once themselves, they probably observed and then plotted the number of coffee sessions versus the amount of research done by the man. Of course they found an inverse correlation . . . and he wasn't given as much of a salary increase as others. Eventually stronger or more negative messages were sent.

You can guess the result. He left and the total output of the department in which he worked went down far more than the loss of one person would dictate. He had been a spark plug in the system for others, a touchstone, a glue for groups, a file of experience, a place to have a laugh and a coffee.

You must afford to have people like this exceptional person in manufacturing development if you are good enough to find them and smart enough to keep them. These touchstones can sometimes find gold even though they are not the sole Masters of a craft that we must expect a manufacturing development Master to be.

♦   ♦

In the project descriptions I had available, there is one visionary project that was rated successful by everyone . . . workers and administrators. It involved an exceptional group. There was no single Master.

It was a project involving many people with individual characteristics similar to those of actors in the Broadway musical *A Chorus Line*. There wasn't a single star but there were touchstones; nor were there many hit songs, but there were obvious successes. It just was good, taken altogether.

I will let you read the description of the Shared Resources Project as written by the lead engineer, John Lubash, and then go on with the metaphor.

Background

Since the mid-1970s, Ford has ever increasingly used programmable devices on the plant floor. "Programmable devices" include computers, programmable logic controllers, computer numerical controllers, and micro-processor controlled equipment which are imbedded in our manufacturing processes to provide better process control. Better process control in turn leads to improved process repeatability which translates into best-in-class quality of our products.

This technology has not only changed the way we do business on the plant floor by providing a window into our manufacturing processes but has given plant floor people a way to manage information flow and improve machine uptime. This change in technology over the last decade can be described as revolutionary because the devices did not appear smoothly over time, but were introduced in several "giant steps", from a few hundred to over thousands. Such huge steps necessitated the development of methodologies for the people in operations to manage and better utilize this technology. Along the way it was concluded that these methodologies had to focus on the integration of people with the technology.

The Shared Resource Process which resulted was a new way of doing business that relied on two basic methodologies known as the "T4 Program" and "Test Tracking."

Technology transfer through teamwork (T4)

The T4 program leverages human resources available from plants and divisions who have a vested interest in the development of plant floor solutions to operational problems. It does this by bringing them together at a neutral site away from the plant and its immediate problems (i.e. the Manufacturing Development Center). It also leverages resources from our suppliers. Suppliers provide the latest technology on consignment knowing that when prototype systems are launched, they will sell "multiple copies" of the hardware and base software. Three items characterize this program:

1. People are the mechanism for technology transfer; technology cannot be just handed-off. As people develop solutions to their operational problems, they imbed the new technology and carry it back to the plant floor.
2. Cross-functional/cross-organizational teams are needed not only for more effective development but also to enable application sharing across components of the company.
3. Efforts are focused on specific problems. People are best motivated out of needs and urgency. All development is aimed at solutions to real-world problems.

Pre-production Staging ("Test Tracking") of plant-bound systems

Test Tracking specifically targets reduction of major launch problems. After functionally replicating the plant floor (hardware, software, and manufacturing process including end effectors), systems are developed, tested and debugged at MDC prior to launch in the target plant. This approach provides a "plug-and-play" environment to develop pin-point solutions.

Taken together, these two components comprise the methodology known as the Shared Resources Process.

The shared resources pilot at MDC

This methodology was piloted at MDC over four years [note added: i.e. mid-1987 through mid-1991]. Eighteen different/new systems were developed and launched during that time, and on the average twenty-five divisional plant personnel from at least four divisions were on-site working on plant floor problems. They were supplemented by over 25 suppliers on-site helping in the development effort. Specific individuals rotated into MDC and then back to operations, but the average composition of personnel remained more or less constant.

Of course, the scope of the pilot evolved from its inception to these levels [note added: see the opening metaphor of the musical]. The implementation of the methodology began with the replication of just one system with a handful of people from one plant. Success with this one system led to more support from the particular divisions (with that plant) and then to more successes. As the benefits of debugging systems in a non-production environment became apparent, additional components and suppliers joined the team, increasing its scope to include:

- Twelve Powertrain applications – each of which was replicated and customized to the needs of the specific plant.

- Four Automotive Components Group applications (different divisions) – some of which used the concepts and approaches already developed in the Powertrain systems.
- Two Body and Assembly applications.

Benefits of the shared resources process

The tangible benefits of the Shared Resources Process could best be understood through examples, but these have a proprietary value and will not be described. Let us just say that in two cases launched recently, the first using the "conventional" method and the second using the Shared Resources Process, the latter saved 24 months.

In the first case, despite excellent project coordination by divisional personnel, the "pieces of technology" developed by the four organizations shown in the attachment [note added: not included] could not be integrated and tested until the system was on the plant floor. Though each of the four had worked from detailed specifications, they worked separately. The computer interfaces, monitoring software, and network communications all ran well individually, but integration and debugging on the plant floor took 24 months. In addition, when the system was up and running, it had little credibility due to the excessive debugging effort.

In the second case, involving different suppliers working on an even more complex system, the development, testing, and debugging took place in one location. The result was a system that got off to an excellent start. The same development steps were employed, but they were accomplished with all parties working together on a daily basis, benefiting from the accumulated development experience of everyone involved.

Cost savings, quality improvements and intangibles

Cost and quality benefits were computed in detail, and healthy estimates were also made as to expected quality improvements.

These alone justified the Shared Resources Process. A significant number of other benefits can, however, be cited as based on the experience gained during the three years of implementing the Shared Resources Process. These include:

- New teams of application developers rotating into the co-located Shared Resources Center benefit from the accrued experiences of their predecessors. They build upon that knowledge to save significant time in developing the next new systems. One estimate of time saved made for just one specific program based on the MDC experience was over 20 man-years saved through the Shared Resources Process.
- In the course of working with technical specialists provided by our suppliers and those internal to the company, many pin-point solutions were developed: for example, protocols to solve the communication problem between disparate hardware platforms.
- The process of co-locating individuals to share resources builds a community which tears down "chimneys", which are lines of communication and decisions restricted to go up through organizations and not across them, and encourages cooperation. It also establishes a directory of names and talents across company components useful for future developmental efforts.
- Three years' post initial growth experience has shown that applications can be shared across divisions having disparate hardware platforms. Philosophies of system design and "pseudo code" (methods for system interfacing) can be transferred effectively, thus saving substantial effort in replication.
- Plant floor systems developed through this process started trouble-free. In many cases, after a 6- to 8-month development period at MDC, systems were literally loaded on a truck, driven to the plant, and started up within 24 hours without a single launch problem.
- Customer acceptance is maximized through this process since the customer is directly involved from "day one" of system

specification and development. No developer goes off on his own to produce what he thinks is needed by the plant.

- Technologies developed by one rotating team are often directly usable or transferrable to the next team through the core team that participates in each round of development. We call it the building of "technology footprints" over a three-year period of piloting the Shared Resources Process.

Comments

The Shared Resources Pilot or the Shared Resources Process or Program (it was known by all these titles fitting under the acronym SRP) was concluded not long after a "fair" where hundreds of visitors came by to see the results of the work as presented by all the individual engineers. It was an impressive, day-long display of results and co-working. Several higher level meetings were held in the company to determine how such a process could be used more widely. After differences of opinion were argued out, everyone agreed that attempts should be made to replicate this visionary process on larger scales elsewhere. One replication is in operation as this is written. Instead of describing this or others I will return to the metaphor for the process, a musical, briefly introduced before this description of touchstones working together.

A group of people working at a summer resort got together because they liked each other and each other's skills. Someone, a touchstone, suggested renting the Old Barn playhouse. They could all take parts and at the same time work on sets or write the music or sell tickets. They were sure people would come. They were right.

It grew slowly because there wasn't much money to advertise and they were amateurs at the start. As time went on more people came, they became more practiced and better, and again more people came. It grew. They painted the Old Barn and yet again more people came. There was money for better sets.

Eventually one intermediary (in the real case, this was me) contacted some producers from the big time, from Broadway, to tell them about the Old Barn musical and persuade them to make a trip to the summer resort. These producers liked what they saw, made an offer that couldn't be refused and bought the rights to it all.

The producers were prominent in their field and they knew that to make money they had to have a big name because although some groups had succeeded without one, success was rare without big names and wasn't sure. So they changed some of the people, including the touchstones. They also knew that a few big songs were usually necessary to make a hit show. So, they added songs and changed things to accommodate them.

As this goes to press there are tryouts in Boston and the musical is scheduled for New York, but the original cast and ideas are gone. It may turn out better than current musicals even though it won't be the same as the production in the Old Barn.

It is rarely possible to enlarge or transfer this kind of pilot or program (or musical) without changing it substantially.

While this seems to go against the nature of manufacturing development success, it doesn't. The people are touchstones not Masters and their roles are different. Recognizing this and building upon it is a responsibility for managers. They must recognize that there can be success for local people in a group process without Masters, but that the success will be different and that the original cast must be prepared to stay at home.

The road to success, the process, is nevertheless the same. Focusing on success. Learning from Masters. Following the prescriptions where possible or developing better ones. Completing the job and going on to the next one.

Success is having another challenge to face.

A LAST THING

I promised no summary. I expressed a lament that I could not give you descriptions of all the wonderful projects completed by the people I worked with. While there is wisdom in omitting hundreds of other things it would be foolish not to acknowledge the people I enjoyed working with.

This book which attempts to capture a mood – the idea of a way to success – could only be developed with the help of my former colleagues:

P. H. Abramowitz	F. W. Belzek	R. J. Caloia
R. D. Abramson	V. A. Bergen	J. T. Carson
R. J. Adams	R. A. Bock	K. W. Casey
A. T. Anderson	B. K. Brandau	E. H. Cervin
B. T. Bajorek	M. Brandt	A. Chandler
R. B. Bartram	C. A. Buczek	Y. F. Chang
J. R. Baughman	D. A. Burdick	G. Chapman
B. J. Becker	J. D. Cabrera	D. J. Chesney

S. Cid	H. Greenwood	T. A. Loch
N. Clay	H. J. Griffore	M. Loo
P. E. Coffman	D. W. Hall	J. J. Lubash
L. G. Colovas	Y. A. Hamidieh	C. M. Mack
J. Colvin	R. G. Hardway	M. J. Maddox
H. L. Chesney	R. Hellner	T. M. Mansour
J. C. Cooper	P. J. Helner	G. Martino
F. R. Cotton	R. Higgs	N. B. Mass
D. T. Courtney	D. L. Horton	J. McAlpine
C. M. Davidson	B. Huang	D. M. McCarthy
M. J. DeCello	J. Huff	G. W. McClure
M. Y. Demeri	T. Hughes	C. O. McHugh
W. Dilay	K. D. Humphrey	C. A. Meyer
J. R. Dixon	R. Hurley	F. M. Migda
D. D. Dodge	A. E. Hyrila	G. J. Mikol
J. F. Dominiak	P. L. Jackson	V. Milenkovic
M. M. Dvonch	A. M. Janotik	M. Milewski
W. Donakowski	H. T. Johnson	M. Miller
D. A. Donovan	J. S. Johnson	T. F. Miniuk
L. E. Ellis	R. Kowalak	D. Mitchell
M. K. Endo	L. P. Kazyak	J. W. Mitchell
W. J. Evans	S. Kaufman	S. Mocarski
R. S. Felcher	F. Kennedy	K. Morrison
W. R. Felcher	J. S. Kepran	D. Moskowitz
C. E. Feltner	F. G. King	I. A. Nagisetty
N. L. Field	R. R. Klann	O. A. Newton
L. G. Gargol	A. R. Kormos	H. Nivi
D. F. Gentle	B. Kovacs	R. M. Nowicki
M. P. Gibbons	K. A. Kuhns	R. Noworyta
B. Gilbert	D. L. Labadie	T. M. O'Malley
D. Gohl	M. M. Larkin	D. Ondrus
J. W. Grant	J. M. Lechnar	S. B. O'Reilly

A. K. Oros
C. Otterstetter
J. R. Panyard
E. P. Papadakis
E. S. Papciak
N. Pappas
J. R. Pawelec
R. C. Petrof
H. Phelps
D. Piercecchi
S. Pohly
A. Pond
A. H. Pravis
R. I. Price
D. Pryzma
C. A. Riopelle
H. D. Robinson, Jr.
K. W. Robinson
M. Roebuck
H. O. Ross
D. Saathoff
F. Sawyer
J. Schneider

D. C. Schowiak
B. Schumacher
W. T. Schwartz
R. A. Sensoli
B. Seth
P. R. Sferro
R. N. Sheets
S. Shmuter
J. Sidor
J. Smarsh
A. G. Smith
M. Soltis
W. Speaker
W. Springer
C. Stephan
C. A. Stickels
D. Strausberg
E. A. Styloglou
J. Sullivan
R. L. Sutherland
B. Takacs
S. Taraman
L. L. Terner
K. D. Thompson

F. M. Tibaudo
P. J. Tocco
M. Torbett
O. Troiani
M. R. Vaughen
S. Varga
D. Wagner
J. G. Walacavage
U. F. Walker
S. A. Weiner
R. Whitbeck
T. E. White
J. Wigger
R. R. Wiggle
R. J. Willerer
K. J. Wilson
B. P. Winter
G. Wlodyga
G. Wolter
D. E. Wunderlich
C. M. Yen
L. Zettel
R. Zurilla

AN APPENDIX WITH MORE LANDMARKS

In eight years there were 52 landmarks identified; I cannot describe some projects/programs that might be still in progress. Nor will I describe proprietary work that, although finished with respect to the development phase, still gives Ford an advantage by being kept confidential. I do not regret these gaps: they are evidence of successes, present and future.

In spite of these restrictions there are still many more that could be described in addition to those in the text. I choose only three more; one plant problem, one new technology and one (huge) vision. They add to and illustrate the intended mood of this book. As set out briefly, they will not bore you with detail.

First the plant problem. You will recognize a familiar cadence and mood (in spite of no explicit account of the technology) as recounted by Tony Mansour.

Introduction

One of our divisions was experiencing several vexing problems (though they were not "dying") during the launch of their new, permanent magnet type starter motor. This new motor provides significant size reduction and weight saving over its older-style predecessor.

After a request for technical assistance, a SWAT team of engineers, representing a broad range of expertise was selected and dispatched by MDC management. (SWAT is an acronym from police forces describing a Special Weapons And Tactics group selected to give a broad range of needed skills.) Then, after many learning weeks which grew into months of getting to know the plant floor people and their problems, one important step was towards a focus on a cutting operation on the motor commutator.

A recommendation was made to consider an alternative under-cutting method that eliminated an alignment problem which had been analyzed to be the stumbling block. The recommendation was accepted, and a young division engineer was assigned to work, on-site at MDC, with me (Tony Mansour) on the joint development program.

Development issues

The initial stage of the development effort was aimed at identifying process parameters and establishing feasibility. Funding was shared. The work was performed to a great degree by using the facilities of several outside manufacturers. A list of process factors was generated and used in DOEs (design of experiment) to establish their relative relevance and optimized levels. As a result of these experiments, a solution was determined that required an invention which is now patent-applied-for. The work was completed in three to four months.

Technology transfer

Throughout the course of development, close contact was maintained with the plant engineers so as to include their input. Periodic progress reports were also made to the sponsoring division management in order to maintain their support. Additionally, a link was established between engineers from this particular division and engineers from another to draw on the latter's experience of working with the same type of technology in a production environment. At the conclusion of the development work, the engineer who was resident for these months at MDC returned to his parent organization. He went with the capability to carry out project implementation and his return was arranged just after the project was jointly presented to the division management who lent their support for a pilot system.

Piloting

The role of MDC for this project was soon reduced to residual technical consultation. Support thereafter was continually provided to division personnel in the following areas:

- Establishing system specifications for procurement.
- Developing a list of candidate system suppliers.
- Presenting the project to the vice president (Technical Affairs) to obtain support funding for a pilot system.

The project was approved and final plant piloting was planned by the division for the latter part of 1992.

Comments

What is to be learned here comes from Tony Mansour's statement, "After many learning weeks which grew into months of getting to know the plant floor people and their problems" balanced with "a solution was determined . . . in three to four months". The many learning weeks took nearly a year, or 3 to 4 times the solution time. This is because the plant was not "dying" but had "vexing" problems. Everything else was done in a classic way, by the Master manufacturing developer, Tony Mansour (who wrote an original and more detailed description of this project), by the division engineer, Harvey Krage, and by all the managements involved. In terms of being a "plant problem" it did not have as good a driver in terms of need, as the one for the Welded Aluminum Driveshaft but it had a better driver than the one for the Dearborn Tool and Die job.

The second example comes from a new idea/technology that had its roots in research, a phase of R&D not described in the text. The people involved had a difficult time with implementation. The program eventually made a profit (associated with the purchase and resale of a Ford subsidiary held for a short time), but it has not influenced vehicle production. The "voice" is a shortened version of a description prepared by John Huff, one of the inventors you will read about.

Origin

In 1977, a project was initiated while we were on Research Staff, aimed at improving the corrosion protection afforded by a phosphate conversion coating. Several studies were carried out to relate the corrosion performance of the paint system to variability in the phosphate conversion coating that is first applied to metal surfaces before painting (i.e. coating weight, morphology, porosity and so on). The early work led to the development of an effective electro-chemical test for measuring phosphate coating porosity, useful in guiding later research towards an improved phosphate coating. Based on our fundamental understanding of the corrosion failure mechanism of paint coatings, we knew that development of a low porosity high alkaline resistant phosphate coating would result in a (dramatic) improvement in the overall corrosion performance of the paint system.

A review of commercial phosphate baths showed that they all contained small amounts of nickel ions. To better understand the effect of nickel, experiments were conducted in commercial nickel-free and nickel-containing phosphate baths, and early results prompted us to examine the effect of incorporating larger concentrations of nickel ions in the bath formulation.

The High Nickel Phosphate project was thus born. In our initial studies, phosphate baths were prepared to cover the range from 20 to 80 mole percent nickel. Panels were painted with a conventional spray primer and salt spray tested. For one particular corrosion test, the results were so amazing we set out to confirm the work. Then, many weeks were spent attempting to reproduce these results with no success.

Fortunately, we had saved a little of the original bath. Chemical analysis showed that a mistake had been made in our bath makeup. The actual composition was 85 mole percent not 80 mole percent as we had originally planned. With this new information, we went back and investigated the composition range from 80 to 98 mole percent nickel.

Hundreds of experiments later we determined the most desirable range for optimum corrosion protection. Other metal cations and mixed bath composition were also investigated. We also worked very diligently and "scientifically" to understand the technology we were dealing with – the fundamentals of the process. Ultimately, four patents were issued; Alkaline Resistant Manganese-Nickel-Zinc Phosphate Conversion Coatings and Method of Application; Alkaline Resistant Phosphate Conversion Coatings; Alkaline Resistant Cobalt-Nickel-Zinc Phosphate Conversion Coatings; Alkaline Resistant Cobalt-Zinc Phosphate Conversion Coatings.

Customer buy-in

In 1982, we presented a project review on the high nickel phosphate to upper management. While this and other presentations generated a great deal of interest it became clear that we simply didn't have a customer. We needed to convince operating parts of the company about the benefits of the new phosphate. We weren't skilled in the "convincing" process, so instead of "living in the plant" we went through a lot of testing in our attempts to get customer buy-in. We even phosphated full-size doors in our laboratory system. That was no easy feat for our research-scale facility. After phosphating, the doors were painted and corrosion tested. Results showed a significant improvement in corrosion protection for the high nickel phosphated doors compared to those phosphated with the then commercial system. Operations were impressed but not convinced. They were (properly) concerned about the production feasibility of the process, its costs, and commercialization. Since Ford Motor Company was not in the business of producing phosphate chemicals, commercialization was a central issue.

Commercialization

It was clear that we needed a commercialization plan which included a phosphate supplier. At that time various efforts were under way to purchase subsidiaries. Parker Chemical, a major phosphate supplier to Ford, was one of them. Parker was subsequently purchased not only as a good business investment but also for the express purpose of commercializing the high nickel phosphate. After purchasing Parker the high nickel phosphate technology and special know-how was transferred to Parker; baths were modified to make them more feasible for production. And then Parker took a business step that surprised us: the new phosphate was priced much above the production one already in use. However necessary, this proved to be a marketing mistake.

Production trial

Several thousand cars were phosphated for service evaluation. Two units from that trial – one phosphated with the high nickel and the other with conventional phosphate – were severely tested with impressive results for the new system, but operations people were not convinced that it was worth the substantial cost penalty. A decision on implementation was deferred until the production trial vehicles were surveyed.

A field survey from the trial was conducted of vehicles that had been in service for 2 to 3 winters showing superior results; operations were impressed but refused to implement. They reasoned that it would be difficult to control the bath. We tried other approaches but, in short, the product was never implemented.

There were several possible reasons for our failure to implement what was considered by all to be a superior phosphate. First and foremost, we never got customer buy-in up front. We didn't learn that both control and assured quality was their prime concern. Instead, we developed the product and then attempted to convince the customer of their need to use the product; a case of a solution looking for a problem. The supplier made a critical mistake in the beginning by pricing the product too high and the cost penalty stayed in the mind of operations people forever, even when prices changed.

We were all looked upon as outsiders seeking a profit, one way or another. Not as team workers. Additionally, as stated, we were unable to convince operations that the process could be controlled in production, as we didn't know just how important this was.

Today, the product is used very successfully in the coil coating industry but not extensively in the auto industry.

Comments

Comments don't seem necessary here, they would intrude. The research workers who became developers through a painful learning process, know today how to do/perform manufacturing development from research through implementation.

The last description is of a vision. It is of a vision developed quite recently by people who had learned from their own experiences and those of others such as the one just described.

The following description was prepared by Pete Sferro.

Origin

Ford's Manufacturing Development Center (MDC) had supported a project called Stereolithography for the development of a new methodology to create plastic parts which were replicas of the CAD (computer-aided design) designs. Once initial success was accomplished with Stereolithography, the director of MDC started querying me, the project leader, for my next development project to "replace" Stereolithography, something he did relentlessly with most lead engineers, regardless of their recent successes, forcing them to stretch. I had to have numerous discussions with other engineers, managers and the director on the integration of technologies with engineering problems and was always told not to worry about the size of the problem.

I drew upon past knowledge from working in Manufacturing Engineering, on the plant shop floor with computer-integrated manufacturing, and CAD, and Stereolithography to develop a solution. The intention (vision) we reached was to provide one single engineer with the ability to perform completely all the engineering functions in product, manufacturing and materials handling engineering.

Technology description

The resulting concept was named Direct Engineering (DE). It is an integration of many different technologies – some from the 1970s, 1980s and 1990s. The direct engineering environment is one which would have an engineer querying a computer system by key word, features description, part name, math equations or generic part family to attain a needed part design, manufacturing process and materials handling designs all at the same time. Then as the engineer makes changes to any single part, the change would be reflected in all associated parts that have an interpendency. Parts would then be created using different "free form fabrication" technologies and directly released into production with all needed changes in a 3D solid CAD model.

The main technologies required for Direct Engineering are formidable, just in names alone: an integration of feature-based databases, group technology, knowledge-based templet databases, solid CAD modeling, parametric design systems, an array of CAE (computer-aided engineering) tools, free form fabricating technologies, and NC (numerically controlled) automatic coding systems and machines.

Customer buy-in early-on or sell later

Initially, Direct Engineering was a soft early-on sell involving the basic concepts with the customers without asking for any involvement, let alone a hard buy-in. The director of MDC presented the concept to the Transmission and Chassis Division operating committee for comments. They are very forward looking and computer-aware but while they indicated that Direct Engineering was something that was needed, they felt that the job was so big and so far into the future before anything could be accomplished, that they would not recommend work "now".

The DE concept was further refined with a few months of hard work and presented to the operating committee of Engine Division who also indicated that such a system was needed but that they felt it was still in the future somewhere. Design work continued on the methodology of DE and Phil Abramowitz (our manager) encouraged me to continue onwards by seeking (for a first time at MDC) outside funding to accomplish the vision of DE.

In July 1991, Scott Staley (Research) and I (Peter Sferro, MDC) hosted a meeting with NCMS's features-based working group in Dearborn. This group from the National Center for Manufacturing Studies had been working over a year trying to define a project to develop CAD features without success. Ford presented DE to the group and suggested to a receptive audience that they adopt it to solve a "real engineering problem". The key idea was to take a describable real problem and let its needs describe how the technologies would have to work together; included in that solution were the feature requirements for CAD.

They agreed to the proposal and NCMS recommended that the group apply for matching funds from the US government under their NIST ATP (advanced technology program). The group (Ford, GM, Texas Instruments, United Technologies, Aries

Technology, Cimflex Teknowledge Corp., Cimplex Corp., ICAD Inc., Parametric Technology Corp., Spatial Technology, Inc. and NCMS) applied for ATP funding.

To support the tasks at Ford and thus the project, participating funding in the ATP program was also asked from Scientific Research Labs and Car Product CAD systems. Everyone except an operating division was contacted to make a commitment to support the project, which they did [note added: remember this was a vision and should not early-on bother the customer]. The operations would participate when required. Ford made a five-year $8.6 million commitment (equal to the others) in September 1991 to support the development of RRM (Rapid Response Manufacturing – the name of the overall proposal) and DE.

Concurrent with these events there was a stroke of luck, Ford reorganized its Transmission and Chassis and Engine divisions into one operation called Powertrain. A new manager there, was developing his own vision to help meet their requirements for World Class Timing (WCT) which turned out be be very close to DE and RRM. After several meetings we agreed to work closely together to accomplish a joint vision for Ford. This was our first customer buy-in. As the vision and program are now unfolding, other activities are becoming aware of it; they understand the vision; they understand the need for it and the technology; and they are joining the commitment to make it happen.

Comments

It is interesting to describe the people involved. Pete Sferro, the lead engineer, comes from a diverse background which encompasses the actual use of numerous high technologies in production environments. He is aggressive, ambitious and aspiring, and is willing to take on challenges even though the scope of the problem may exceed his resources. He will be complimented by this description. He is a Master. Phil Abramowitz, the manager at the time, was the coach, patiently and encouragingly helping to resolve various issues through one-on-one meetings addressing technologies, manpower, financing, legal and general support. He worked as a Master before he became a manager.

The key was for management always to project a positive environment. If the vision, the technology and the project are sound, regardless of the size of problems, the engineer can be assured that he will be successful in the quest to advance beyond the operating culture of the time. Management must open the right doors, when needed, to attain support and approval for programs.

This particular program is a vision and yet it started with implementation as the main goal. (Another example showing that the observations provide prescriptions, not rules.) The final test will occur some years from now in the actual building of production parts in the production plant. By that time the vision will probably have been changed several times and surely will have been narrowed down to apply to one new idea.

Each member of the consortium of large and different companies agreed to involve their production people in the program. At Ford, Powertrain has committed to build one particular part and is involving engineers from all disciplines in determining how the system should work, in determining its requirements, and eventually in laying out launch plans.

How different it is, when you have a customer and when the customer works with you. How different it is when you forget who is the seller and who is the buyer. How different it is when you are all on one team.

Winners have teams that act as one.